NEW WORKS
IN ACCOUNTING
HISTORY

Richard P. Brief, *Series Editor*

Leonard N. Stern School of Business
New York University

A Garland Series

INTERNAL ACCOUNTING CONTROL EVALUATION AND AUDITOR JUDGMENT

An Anthology

Theodore J. Mock
and
Jerry L. Turner

Garland Publishing, Inc.
A member of the Taylor & Francis Group
New York & London 1999

Published in 1999 by
Garland Publishing Inc.
A Member of the Taylor & Francis Group
19 Union Square West
New York, NY 10003

10   9   8   7   6   5   4   3   2   1

Library of Congress Cataloging-in-Publication Data

Internal accounting control evaluation and auditor judgment : an anthology /
    Theodore J. Mock, Jerry L. Turner.
        p. cm. — (New works in accounting history)
        An update of Internal accounting control evaluation and auditor judg-
    ment / by Theodore J. Mock and Jerry L. Turner. c.1981.
        Includes bibliographical references.
        ISBN 0-8153-3443-5 (alk. paper)
        1. Auditing, Internal. I. Mock, Theodore J. II. Turner, Jerry L. (Jerry
    Lynn). 1942–   . III. Mock, Theodore J. Internal accounting control evalua-
    tion and auditor judgment. IV. Series.
    HF5668.25.M6 1999
    657'.458—dc21   99-36251

Printed on acid-free, 250-year-life paper
Manufactured in the United States of America

Contents

Preface to the Anthology

This anthology presents the results of a comprehensive empirical study of internal control evaluation and auditor judgment initiated by Peat, Marwick, Mitchell & Co. in 1977 and originally published as a AICPA research monograph in 1981. The research consisted of a series of five field experiments and a related verbal protocol study. The experimental task involved audit program planning given a comprehensive set of audit workpapers. The AICPA monograph won the American Accounting Association Wildman Award in 1982.

This anthology extends the original AICPA monograph in the following ways:

- An updated review of the professional literature has been integrated into Chapter 2.

- The original statistical results which were based primarily on univariate analyses have been augmented based on the multivariate analyses performed by Theodore Mock and Paul Watkins in 1982. These results are now presented in Chapter 9.

- The process tracing (verbal protocol) results in Chapter 11 have been revised to include additional decision process analyses published in Stanley Biggs and Theodore Mock in 1983 and also an analysis of the criteria utilized by the auditors as described in Stanley Biggs and Theodore Mock in 1989.

- The Summary, Implications, and Implementation chapter has been augmented to include the new results and implications now contained in Chapters 9 and 11. Also, we now discuss the implementation of the research; that is, how the development of SEADOC at PMM (now KPMG Peat Marwick) was related to the research published in the original AICPA monograph.

In addition to the acknowledgments published in the original monograph (see pp. xi), we would like to acknowledge the important contributions of Stanley Biggs, Paul Watkins and John Willingham, each of whom co-authored works which provided some of the results which have been incorporated into this anthology. Helpful secretarial support was provided by Ingrid McClendon at the Levanthal School of Accounting, University of Southern California and able research assistance was provided by Charlene Pea Choo See at the Center for Accounting and Auditing Research, Nanyang Technological University. To each of the above, we express our sincere gratitude.

Theodore J. Mock
Palos Verdes, California
Jerry L. Turner
Memphis, Tennessee

Foreword to Original AICPA Publication

This is the third in the auditing research monograph series published by the Auditing Standards Division of the American Institute of Certified Public Accountants. The series was undertaken in the belief that research would be helpful in approaching and solving significant practice problems related to the audit function.

One of the primary objectives behind publishing Auditing Research Monograph 3 is to stimulate additional research pertaining to matters of interest to the Auditing Standards Board. I believe that *Internal Accounting Control Evaluation and Auditor Judgment* will achieve this objective.

In my opinion, this monograph represents a highly valuable contribution to the accounting profession. Using sound research methods, the monograph addresses a pervasive practice problem. Moreover, its authors combine the research methodological skills of academicians with the problem identification skills of practitioners.

New York   Dan M. Guy
December 1980   Director of Auditing Research

Preface to Original Publication

This monograph summarizes selected portions of a comprehensive empirical study of internal accounting control evaluation and auditor judgment. The study was initiated by Peat, Marwick, Mitchell & Co. And was undertaken by the Audit Research Group, Department of Professional Practice—Accounting and Auditing. We are indebted to Peat, Marwick Mitchell & Co. For sponsoring the research and in particular to Dr. Richard B. Lea (now on the faculty of Boston University) and Mr. Robert K. Elliott for initiating the project and providing criticism and assistance during its execution. Ms. Susan Sporer provided valuable research assistance, particularly in the content analysis phase of the study, and Peter D. Jacobson provided useful editorial comments.

One research element was a protocol study of auditor decision-making, which was conducted with the able assistance of Dr. Stanley F. Biggs of the University of Wisconsin, Madison. Research assistance on the latter portions of the research was provided by Ms. Deanna A. Daniels of the University of Southern California through the Center for Accounting Research.

To each of the above, we wish to express our sincere gratitude. In addition, we would like to acknowledge the American Institute of Certified Public Accountants and Douglas R. Carmichael for providing the means for publishing the research results.

Theodore J. Mock   Palos Verdes, California
Jerry L. Turner   Denver, Colorado

Internal Accounting Control Evaluation and Auditor Judgment

CHAPTER 1

Introduction and Overview

Under present generally accepted auditing standards, auditors study and evaluate internal accounting control to determine the nature, extent, and timing of audit procedures that must be performed in developing an opinion on the financial statements. However, there are no explicit professional guidelines to apply when making such determinations. When this study was begun, little was known about how auditors make such judgments, yet they are fundamental to an audit.

Understanding the auditor's judgment process may lead to methods of aiding the auditor in evaluating audit evidence. It seems unlikely that significant improvements will be forthcoming without some general agreement on how auditors reach decisions about how much audit evidence is appropriate in different internal control situations. When the study was conducted, there certainly was no general agreement.

In fact, early research findings raised some puzzling issues. Ronald A.G. Weber found, for example, that even though a simulation decision aid improved auditors' perceptions of a system's error characteristics (their perceptions were more accurate), the decision aid had no significant effect on their subsequent audit plan.[1] Edward J. Joyce, on the other hand, found that "different auditors might agree on the quality of internal control in a given situation, yet disagree on how to incorporate that evaluation in a judgment of what audit work to plan and perform.[2] As a result, their recommendations varied widely.

Because of the importance of evaluating internal accounting controls and limited previous research, an extensive research project was designed and implemented. The primary purpose of the project was to obtain empirical evidence on the effect of changes in internal accounting controls and differences in guidance on auditors' decisions on the extent of audit tests. Specifically, the research was intended to address the following kinds of questions:

- Do auditors respond to different evidence of the effectiveness of internal controls by effecting corresponding changes in sample size recommendations for audit tests?
- Do they consider the same factors (cues) in making their decisions?
- Of the cues they perceive as influencing their decisions, which do they reference most frequently, and which are statistically related to their decisions?
- Are their decisions influenced by explicit guidance on appropriate decision considerations?
- What behavioral factors and heuristics influence their judgment process?
- What decision processes are utilized in completing this task?
- Are auditor decisions best modeled in terms of simple linear models or by more complex configural information processing models?
- How can audit practice be augmented with obtained research results?

These questions and others are addressed in detail in the following chapters of this anthology. However, some of the more significant findings of the research are as follows: Auditors do respond systematically to different evidence of the effectiveness of internal accounting controls. Specifically, when given improved compliance test results, they increased their reliance and reduced the related extent of substantive tests. However, a great deal of variability among auditors is observed in both the specific sample sizes recommended and in the underlying rationale given for those sample sizes. The complexity of the internal accounting control evaluation task was evident in two significant areas. First, many factors were identified in the subject's sample size rationale documentation. Second, variation was observed in their interpretation of these various factors, such as the nature of the audit test, the relevance of the internal accounting control strengths, and the amount of reliance they were willing to place on those controls. The research also permitted the study of various other factors, such as the effect of providing the auditor with explicit guidance; the effect of various behavioral factors; and the effect of adding a review by a supervising manager to the decision process.

NOTES

1. Ronald A.G. Weber, "Auditor Decision Making: A Study of Some Aspects of Accuracy and Consensus, and the Usefulness of a Simulation Decision Aid for Assessing Overall System Reliability" (Ph.D. diss., University of Minnesota, 1977).

2. Edward J. Joyce, "Expert Judgment in Audit Program Planning," *Studies on Human Information Processing in Accounting,* Supplement to vol. 14 of the *Journal of Accounting Research* (1976): 53.

CHAPTER 2

The Development of Professional Standards Related to Internal Accounting Control Evaluation

Although the study and evaluation of internal accounting controls may appear to be a problem of fairly recent development, auditors have contended with the problem for over three-quarters of a century. Since the early part of the twentieth century, auditors have taken internal accounting control systems into account when designing audit programs. As early as 1917, Robert H. Montgomery noted that "if the auditor has satisfied himself that the system of internal check is adequate, he will not attempt to duplicate work which has been properly performed by someone else."[1]

Of course, such reviews of internal accounting controls were not required by professional standards, and no formalized guidance really existed. Audit testing developed initially because of the inability to cope with increased transaction volume. It was not until after the McKesson and Robbins investigation that the impetus existed to require the auditor to relate the evaluation of internal accounting controls to the extent of other testing. This should be borne in mind when the following summary of early literature is reviewed.

EARLY LITERATURE

One of the earliest references in professional auditing literature to the need to review internal accounting control was in the 1929 publication titled *Verification of Financial Statements (Rev.)*. This was a revision by the American Institute of Accountants of a pamphlet printed in the April 1917 issue of the Federal Reserve Bulletin and reprinted in 1918 for general distribution under the title *Approved Methods for the Preparation of Balance-Sheet Statements*. The first paragraph stated the following:

> The scope of the work indicated in these instructions includes a verification of the assets and liabilities of a business enterprise at a given date, a verification of the profit-and-loss account for the period under review, and, incidentally, an examination of the accounting system for the purpose of ascertaining the effectiveness of the internal check.[2]

The pamphlet briefly approached the relationship between internal accounting control ("internal check") and the audit program further in the first paragraph:

> The extent of the verification will be determined by the conditions in each concern. In some cases the auditor may find it necessary to verify a substantial portion or all of the transactions recorded upon the books. In others, where the system of internal check is good, tests only may suffice. The responsibility for the extent of the work required must be assumed by the auditor.[3]

In 1936 a revision of the 1929 pamphlet was prepared by the American Institute of Accountants and was published by the Federal Reserve Board under the title *Examination of Financial Statements by Independent Public Accountants*. In this publication the importance of internal accounting control evaluation was emphasized in the first sentence:

> This pamphlet deals with the accountant's examination of the balance sheet of a business enterprise at a specified date and of the profit and loss and surplus accounts for the period under review, and also with his review of the accounting procedure for the purpose of ascertaining the accounting principles followed and the adequacy of the system of internal check and control.[4]

It was in the 1936 pamphlet that internal control was defined for the first time:

The term "internal check and control" is used to describe those measures and methods adopted within the organization itself to safeguard the cash and other assets of the company as well as to check the clerical accuracy of the bookkeeping. The safeguards will cover such matters as the handling of incoming mail and remittances, the proceeds of cash sales, the preparation and payment of payrolls and the disbursement of funds generally, and the receipt and shipment of goods. These safeguards will frequently take the form of a definite segregation of duties or the utilization of mechanical devices.[5]

The pamphlet emphasized the judgments required on the part of the auditor in restricting audit tests on the basis of effective accounting controls. The pamphlet also suggested audit procedures the auditor should consider if the system of internal check and control was not adequate.

DEVELOPMENT OF STANDARDS

By 1939 the auditing profession had grown rapidly. The American Institute of Accountants, realizing that the complexities of modern businesses were increasing the diversity of conditions encountered by the auditor, formed its committee on auditing procedure. The task of the committee was to review auditing procedures and related questions. Instead of revising previous documents, the committee chose to issue Statements on Auditing Procedure (SAPs), which either modified or superseded parts of the 1936 pamphlet.

Statement on Auditing Procedure 1, *Extensions of Auditing Procedure,* issued in 1939, presented some of the underlying concepts of the auditing profession that later became a framework for generally accepted auditing standards. One of the concepts discussed was that of internal accounting control evaluation:

It is the duty of the independent auditor to review the system of internal check and accounting control so as to determine the extent to which he considers that he is entitled to rely upon it.[6]

Statement on Auditing Procedure 1 also provided a recommended report form, which, in the first paragraph, described the scope of the examination, including a specific reference to the system of internal control. The wording of the paragraph was not mandatory, however, and many auditors deleted the reference to the system of internal control in their reports.

The Securities and Exchange Commission (SEC) recognized the importance of the auditor's relationship with internal control evaluation in 1940, when it issued Regulation S-X. This regulation stated that the independent auditor was permitted to give due weight "to an internal system of audit regularly maintained by means of auditors employed on the registrant's own staff."[7] Regulation S-X was amended in 1941 to require that "in determining the scope of the audit necessary, appropriate consideration shall be given to the adequacy of the system of internal check and control."[8]

In 1947 the committee on auditing procedure reiterated its requirement that auditors use their study and evaluation of internal accounting controls to guide their planned testing. The special report, titled *Tentative Statement of Auditing Standards--Their Generally Accepted Significance and Scope,* defined auditing standards grouped as (1) general standards, (2) standards of field work, and (3) standards of reporting. The second standard of field work was as follows:

There is to be a proper study and evaluation of the existing internal control as a basis for reliance thereon and for the determination of the resultant extent of the tests to which auditing procedures are to be restricted.[9]

The report also included a discussion of the auditor's study and evaluation of internal controls, including the role of testing such controls and the need for auditors' judgments in evaluating the controls.

The membership of the Institute approved the report summary of auditing standards in September 1948.[10] A year later, at the 1949 annual meeting, the membership approved Statement on Auditing Procedure 23, which was later incorporated in the formal standards as the fourth standard of reporting.

The approval of auditing standards created a need for a modification of the standard report. Because such a report was assumed to be issued within the framework of generally accepted auditing standards, certain phrases were deemed superfluous. As a result, Statement on Auditing Procedure 24 was issued, which amended the report by excluding any reference to the examination of the system of internal control and to the omission of a detailed audit of the transactions.

REFINING THE DEFINITION

In 1949 the committee on auditing procedure published the results of an analytical study that was "directed particularly to the consideration of the nature and characteristics of internal control and to the delineation of the respective spheres of interest and responsibility of management and the public accountant. . . ."[11] This study discussed the elements of a properly coordinated system, reported on the relationships of management and the public accountant to the internal control system, and provided a graphic illustration of internal control.

The report indicated that the public accountant's review of the system of internal control had two potential benefits. First, the review would enable the auditor to determine the reliance that could be placed on the system and, by adjusting other audit procedures accordingly, an opinion on the financial statements could be expressed. Second, where the review indicated apparent weaknesses, recommendations for possible corrective measures could be conveyed to management. In connection with the secondary aspect of the review, the report indicated that the effectiveness of the organizational plan, the division of responsibilities, and such special control procedures as budgetary controls, reports, analyses, and cost systems were among the areas that the public accountant should review.

Experience over the next few years determined that the definition provided in the 1949 *Internal Control* report was not easily interpreted and, possibly, placed greater responsibility on the auditor than might be required under generally accepted auditing standards. Accordingly, in 1958 the committee on auditing procedure issued SAP 29, *Scope of the Independent Auditor's Review of Internal Control*. In SAP 29, the committee reiterated that the selection of auditing procedures, the timing of such procedures, and the determination of the extent to which they should be followed depended largely on the auditor's judgment of the adequacy and effectiveness of the internal controls. Such judgment resulted from the study and evaluation, including testing, observation, investigation, and inquiry, of those internal controls that appeared to influence the reliability of the financial records. The committee indicated that accounting controls generally bore directly and importantly on the reliability of financial records and would, therefore, require evaluation. Administrative controls, on the other hand, ordinarily related only indirectly to the financial records and thus would not require evaluation but could be evaluated in some particular circumstances.[12]

In 1963 the committee on auditing procedure issued SAP 33, *Auditing Standards and Procedures,* which consolidated and replaced the following previous pronouncements: *Internal Control* (1949), *Generally Accepted Auditing Standards* (1954), *Codification of Statements on Auditing Procedure* (1951), and SAPs 25-32 (issued on various dates after 1951). Statement on Auditing Procedure 33 essentially was a codification of earlier committee pronouncements.

The next authoritative pronouncement on the evaluation of internal controls was SAP 49, *Reports on Internal Control,* issued in 1971. This statement recognized that auditors were furnishing reports on their evaluations of internal control for use by management, regulatory agencies, other independent auditors, and the general public. Because of the technical nature and complexity of internal accounting control and the consequent problem of understanding reports thereon, questions had been raised about whether such reports served a useful purpose for all people to whom they might be issued.[13] The committee concluded that if such reports were issued the risk of misunderstanding could be reduced by adopting a form of report that described in reasonable detail the objective and limitations of internal accounting control and the auditor's evaluation of it.

Statement on Auditing Procedure 49 was supplemented in 1972 by SAP 52, *Reports on Internal Control Based on Criteria Established by Governmental Agencies.* Statement on Auditing Procedure 52 dealt more specifically with reports on internal control based on "criteria established by agencies in reasonable detail and in terms susceptible to objective application."[14] The statement specifically allowed the auditor to express a conclusion based on the agencies' criteria, concerning the adequacy of the procedures studied. The auditor's report also could identify any condition that was believed not to be in conformity with such criteria and that was determined to be a material weakness.

In reviewing the auditor's study and evaluation of internal control, SAP 54 reiterated that the purposes were to establish a basis for reliance thereon and to determine the nature, extent, and timing of audit tests to be applied to the examination of the financial statements. Although the study and evaluation made for such purposes frequently provided a basis for constructive suggestions to clients concerning improvements in internal control, and such suggestions were desirable, the scope of any additional study to develop such suggestions was not covered by generally accepted auditing standards. The committee reiterated that accounting control, but not administrative control, was within the scope of the study and evaluation of internal control contemplated by generally accepted auditing standards.

RELATING ACCOUNTING CONTROLS
TO THE AUDIT PROGRAM

Statement on Auditing Procedure 54 noted the following:

Adequate evaluation of a system of internal control requires (a) knowledge and understanding of the procedures and methods prescribed and (b) a reasonable degree of assurance that they are in use and are operating as planned.[15]

The information necessary for the first requirement ordinarily would be obtained through discussion with appropriate client personnel and reference to such documents as procedure manuals, job descriptions, flowcharts, and decision tables. Such information could be recorded in the form of answers to a questionnaire, narrative memorandums, flowcharts, decision tables, or any other form that would suit the auditor's needs or preferences.

The information needed for the second requirement would be obtained through compliance tests. If compliance tests are required, the statement indicates that "What constitutes a 'reasonable' degree of assurance is a matter of auditing judgment; the 'degree of assurance' necessarily depends on the nature, timing, and extent of the tests and on the results obtained."[16]

Statement on Auditing Procedure 54 provided a "conceptually logical approach" to the evaluation of accounting control, which focused directly on the purpose of preventing or detecting material errors and irregularities in financial statements. Under this approach, the following steps should be applied in considering each significant class of transactions and related balances to be audited:

a. Consider the types of errors and irregularities that could occur.
b. Determine the accounting control procedures that should prevent or detect such errors and irregularities.
c. Determine whether the necessary procedures are prescribed and are being followed satisfactorily.
d. Evaluate any weaknesses—i.e., types of potential errors and irregularities not covered by existing control procedures—to determine their effect on (1) the nature, timing, or extent of auditing procedures to be applied and (2) suggestions to be made to the client.[17]

It was pointed out that the auditor's review of the accounting control system and the compliance tests should be related to the purposes of the evaluation of the system. For this reason, "generalized or overall evaluations are not useful for auditors because they do not help the auditor decide the extent to which auditing procedures may be restricted." For each significant class of transactions and related balances, the conclusion reached from the evaluation of accounting control should be whether the prescribed procedures and compliance with them are satisfactory. They may be considered satisfactory if no conditions believed to be material weaknesses are discovered.

Statement on Auditing Procedure 54 also discussed the relationship between the evaluation of internal accounting control and the extent of other auditing procedures to be performed. The statement indicated that the ultimate purpose of evaluating internal accounting control is to contribute to the "reasonable basis for an opinion" comprehended in the third standard of field work.

In discussing this relationship, two important topics were covered: the type of evidence needed to satisfy the third standard and the fact that complete reliance on internal accounting control is not appropriate. Statement on Auditing Procedure 54 indicates, "the evidential matter required by the third standard is obtained through two general classes of auditing procedures: (a) tests of details of transactions and balances and (b) analytical review of significant ratios and trends and resulting investigation of unusual fluctuations and questionable items. These procedures are referred to in this Statement as 'substantive tests.'"[18] The purpose of substantive procedures is to "obtain evidence as to the validity and the propriety of accounting treatment of transactions and balances or, conversely, of errors or irregularities therein. Although this purpose differs from that of compliance tests, both purposes often are accomplished concurrently through tests of details."[19]

In regard to how much reliance can be placed on internal accounting controls, it was stated that with respect to material amounts the auditor should not place *complete* reliance to the exclusion of other auditing procedures. Complete reliance was not suggested in either the second or third standards of field work, nor would it be appropriate because of the inherent limitations in any system of internal accounting control. Statement on Auditing Procedure 54 also indicated that (1) work by internal auditors should be considered as a supplement to, but not as a substitute for, tests by independent auditors and (2) that statistical sampling may be a practical means for expressing in quantitative terms the auditor's judgment concerning the reliance to be derived from substantive tests and for determining sample size and evaluating sample results.

Additional pronouncements dealing with different aspects of internal accounting control were issued subsequent to SAP 54. Statement on Auditing Standards (SAS) 3—*The Effects of EDP on the Auditor's Study and Evaluation of Internal Control,* indicated that the evaluation of the EDP aspects of a system of accounting control is not different conceptually from the evaluation of other aspects of the system and therefore should be an integral part of the auditor's evaluation of the system. Statement on Auditing Standards 9—*The Effect of an Internal Audit Function on the Scope of the Independent Auditor's Examination,* indicated that "when the independent author considers the work of internal auditors in determining the nature, timing, and extent of his own audit procedures or when internal auditors provide direct assistance in the performance of his work, judgments as to the effectiveness of internal accounting control, sufficiency of tests performed, materiality of transactions, and other matters affecting his report on the financial statements must be those of the independent auditor." [20]

Statement on Auditing Standards 20—*Required Communication of Material Weaknesses in Internal Accounting Control,* established the requirement that the auditor communicate to senior management and to the board of directors or its audit committee the material weaknesses in internal accounting control identified during an examination of financial statements made in accordance with generally accepted auditing standards. Prior to SAS 20 the issuance of such reports was optional.

FURTHER DEVELOPMENT OF
PROFESSIONAL STANDARDS

Subsequent to completion of the field experiment, numerous professional standards relating to internal accounting control issues were issued. Statement on Auditing Standards No. 30 - *Reporting on Internal Accounting Control*[21] responded to the need for guidance as to written reports on a client's internal control structure. Such reports often are requested by management, an organization's board of directors, or an organization's audit committee. Additionally, third parties, such as prospective investors, prospective creditors, or regulatory agencies often require such reports. In that regard, SAS No. 30 indicated that the accountant can be engaged to:

1. Express an opinion on internal control structure as of a particular date or during a particular time.
2. Report on all or part of internal control structure based on the preestablished criteria of a regulatory agency.
3. Issue special-purpose reports on all or part of an organization's internal control structure for restricted use of management or a particular third party.

SAS No. 30 emphasized that in cases where the accountant is engaged to issue an opinion on an organization's internal control structure, the scope of the examination will be greater than that required for an audit conducted under generally accepted auditing standards. The pronouncement provided a suggested form for reporting an unqualified opinion, as well as a suggested additional paragraph if one or more material weaknesses are discovered.

SAS No. 39 - *Audit Sampling*[22] introduced the concept of audit risk into the official literature. In that pronouncement, audit risk was defined to be:

> The allowable audit risk that monetary misstatements equal to tolerable misstatement might remain undetected for the account balance or class of transactions and related assertions after the auditor has completed all audit procedures deemed necessary.[23]

The definition of audit risk (AR) was formalized into a model identifying four separate components of that risk:

$$AR = IR \times CR \times AP \times TD$$

where: IR = Inherent Risk is the susceptibility of an assertion to a material misstatement assuming there are no related internal control structure policies or procedures.

CR = Control Risk is the risk that a material misstatement that could occur in an assertion will not be prevented or detected on a timely basis by the entity's internal control structure policies and procedures. The auditor may assess control risk at the maximum, or assess control risk below the maximum based on the sufficiency of evidential matter obtained to support the effectiveness of internal control structure policies or procedures. The quantification for this model relates to the auditor's evaluation of the overall effectiveness of those internal control structure policies or procedures that would prevent or detect material misstatements equal to tolerable misstatement in the related account balance or class of transactions. For example, if the auditor believes that pertinent control structure policies or procedures would prevent or detect misstatements equal to tolerable misstatement about half the time, he would assess this risk at 50 percent.

AP = The auditor's assessment of the risk that analytical procedures and other relevant substantive tests would fail to detect misstatements that could occur in an assertion equal to tolerable misstatement, given that such misstatements occur and are not detected by the internal control structure.

TD = The allowable risk of incorrect acceptance for the substantive test of details, given that misstatements equal to tolerable misstatement occur in an assertion and are not detected by the internal control structure or analytical procedures and other relevant substantive tests.

SAS No. 39 emphasized that the model was not intended to be a mathematical formula including all factors that may influence the determination of individual risk components; however, the pronouncement indicated that some auditors find such a model to be useful when planning appropriate risk levels for audit procedures to achieve the auditor's desired audit risk.

SAS No. 39 provided more explicit guidance than had been apparent in earlier pronouncements:

> When designing samples for tests of controls the auditor ordinarily should plan to evaluate operating effectiveness in terms of deviations from prescribed internal control structure policies or procedures, as to either the rate of such deviations or the monetary amount of the related transactions. In this context pertinent internal control structure policies or procedures are ones that, had they not been included in the design of the internal control structure would have adversely affected the auditor's planned assessed level of control risk.[24]

> The auditor should determine the maximum rate of deviations from the prescribed internal control structure policy and procedure that he would be willing to accept without altering his planned assessed level of control risk. This is the *tolerable rate*. In determining the tolerable rate, the auditor should consider (a) the planned assessed level of control risk, and (b) the degree of assurance desired by the evidential matter in the sample...[25]

SAS No. 39 further described the manner in which the tolerable rate is to be used:

> If the auditor concludes that the sample results do not support the planned assessed level of control risk for an assertion, he should reevaluate the nature, timing, and extent of substantive procedures based on a revised consideration of the assessed level of control risk for the relevant financial statement assertions.[26]

Although SAS No. 39 indicated that establishment of the tolerable rate depends on the judgment of the auditor, examples were provided using tolerable rates of approximately five to ten percent.

In 1983, SAS No. 47 - *Audit Risk and Materiality in Conducting an Audit*[27] was issued. The pronouncement differed from SAS No. 39 in two ways. First, SAS No. 47 more explicitly described the inverse relationship between audit risk and materiality. Second, SAS No. 47 required the auditor to "...consider audit risk at the individual account-balance or class-of-transactions level because such consideration directly assists him in determining the scope of auditing procedures for the balance or class and related assertions." The components of audit risk were identified as inherent risk, control risk, and detection risk, but these components were not shown as a mathematical formula as in Appendix A of SAS No. 39. The definitions of control risk were substantially the same in both pronouncements.

In response to technological changes affecting the processing of accounting data, SAS No. 48 - *The Effects of Computer Processing on the Audit of Financial Statements*[28] was issued. This pronouncement identified internal accounting controls specific to electronic data processing (EDP) as general controls and application controls.

SAS No. 55 - *Consideration of the Internal Control Structure in a Financial Statement Audit*[29] was issued as one of the "Expectation Gap" standards. This was the first audit pronouncement since SAP No. 47, issued in 1972, to focus entirely on the impact of internal control structure policies or procedures on audit programs and auditor's opinions. It also provided the greatest detail regarding the factors that should be considered by the auditor.

SAS No. 55 indicated that "an entity's internal control structure consists of three elements: the control environment, the accounting system, and control procedures."[30]

SAS No. 60 - *Communication of Internal Control Structure Related Matters Noted in an Audit*[31] superseded SAS No. 20 and selected portions of SAS No. 30. SAS No. 60 indicates (1) that the auditor's communication can be either written or oral, although written is preferable, and (2) the auditor should not issue a written communication when no reportable conditions are noted.

SAS No. 65 - *The Auditor's Consideration of the Internal Audit Function in an Audit of Financial Statements*[32] discusses the matters that should be considered by the independent auditor in evaluating whether the work of the internal auditors can be relied upon to some extent in the audit examination. SAS No. 65 notes that, in some cases, the work of the internal auditors may be either not relevant to the independent auditor's examination or not cost-efficient to evaluate. However, if the independent auditor believes that the work of the internal audit function is relevant, the competence and objectivity of the internal audit function must be evaluated.

If the internal audit function is judged to be both competent and objective, the effect of the internal auditor's work on the audit engagement should be considered. It is important to note that it is the responsibility of the independent auditor to audit the financial statements.

The independent auditor should evaluate and test the effectiveness of the internal auditor's work by examining the same or similar controls, transactions, or balances examined by the internal audit function. Any significant differences in the results obtained by the two groups of auditors would indicate that less reliance should be placed on the internal auditor's work.

In 1985, The National Commission on Fraudulent Financial Reporting, known as the Treadway Commission, was formed to identify causative factors of fraudulent reporting. Among the findings of the Commission was that in many of the audit failures of the 1980s, the companies had received clean audit opinions and that internal controls were considered adequate by both external and internal auditors. Among the issues raised as a result of these findings was the need for requiring an attestation on internal control.

Despite the need for separate attestation on internal control, there was general disagreement about what constituted a suitable model against which an attestation could be made. In 1987, the Treadway Commission called for a study to develop a common definition of internal control and a general framework. To accomplish this, the Committee of Sponsoring Organizations of the Treadway Commission, know as COSO[33], selected Coopers & Lybrand to perform the study.

The results of a three year study were published in 1992 as *Internal Control — Integrated Framework*,[34] now referred to as the COSO study. In 1994, the GAO endorsed the report and in December, 1995, the

AICPA issued *SAS No. 78 - Consideration of Internal Control in a Financial Statement Audit: An Amendment to SAS No. 55.*[35]

In SAS No. 78, the following definition of internal control is provided:

> Internal control is a process—effected by an entity's board of directors, management, and other personnel—designed to provide reasonable assurance regarding the achievement of objectives in the following categories: (a) reliability of financial reporting, (b) effectiveness and efficiency of operations, and (c) compliance with applicable laws and regulations.

Internal control consists of the following five interrelated components:

a. *Control environment* sets the tone of an organization, influencing the control consciousness of its people. It is the foundation for all other components of internal control, providing discipline and structure.

b. *Risk assessment* is the entity's identification and analysis of relevant risks to achievement of its objectives, forming a basis for determining how the risks should be managed.

c. *Control activities* are the policies and procedures that help ensure that management directives are carried out.

d. *Information and communication* are the identification, capture, and exchange of information in a form and time frame that enable people to carry out their responsibilities.

e. *Monitoring* is a process that assesses the quality of internal control performance over time.[36]

In discussing the Financial Reporting Objective, SAS No. 78 states:

> Generally, controls that are relevant to an audit pertain to the entity's objective of preparing financial statements for external purposes that are fairly presented in conformity with generally accepted accounting principles or a comprehensive basis of accounting other than generally accepted accounting principles.[37]

However, SAS No. 78 also indicates that "controls relating to operations and compliance objectives may be relevant to an audit if they pertain to data the auditor evaluates or uses in applying auditing procedures."[38] Examples include production data used in analytical procedures, and compliance with income tax laws and procedures. The Statement also states that "Internal control over safeguarding of assets against unauthorized acquisition, use, or disposition may include controls relating to financial reporting and operations objectives."[39]

In discussing the relationship of the internal control structure and the audit plan, SAS No. 78 states:

> In all audits, the auditor should obtain an understanding of each of the five components of internal control sufficient to plan the audit by performing procedures to understand the design of controls relevant to an audit of financial statements, and whether they have been placed in operation.[40]

The statement does not specify the manner in which the understanding must be made and does not specify that controls must be tested.

Further emphasis on the importance of internal controls was provided when, in December, 1996, the AICPA issued *SAS No. 80 - Amendment of Statement on Auditing Standards No. 31, Evidential Matter*.[41] This pronouncement considers the impact of computers both on the manner in which audit clients capture, process, and store accounting information and on the nature of evidence available to the auditor. SAS No. 80 states:

> Because of the growth in the use of computers and other information technology, many entities process significant information electronically. Accordingly, it may be difficult or impossible for the auditor to access certain information for inspection, inquiry, or confirmation without using information technology.[42]

The new statement includes examples of evidential matter that may be in electronic form and indicates that an auditor should consider the time during which such evidential matter exists or is available in determining the nature, timing and extent of substantive tests.

In regard to internal accounting controls, the statement indicates that an auditor may determine that in certain engagement environments where evidential matter is in electronic form, it would not be practical or possible to reduce detection risk to an acceptable level by performing only substantive tests. The SAS indicates that in such circumstances, an auditor should perform tests of controls to support an assessed level of control risk below the maximum for affected assertions.

SUMMARY

This chapter has presented a summary of relevant official pronouncements including those issued since completion of the original experiment. Such pronouncements continue to emphasize the importance of the internal accounting control system and the relationship of that system to audit program design. While the overall relationship of reliance on a client's control system and the auditor's substantive audit procedures hasn't been changed by these pronouncements, the framework for analyzing the relationship has been formalized.

Changes in the audit approach to evidence examination due to the transition from primarily manual accounting systems to primarily computer-based accounting systems has been addressed in several pronouncements. Because of the nature of electronic data processing, the auditor no longer may rely solely on substantive procedures when auditing financial statements; instead, the auditor must place some degree of reliance on EDP controls in order to provide a reasonable basis for an opinion.

NOTES

1. Robert H. Montgomery, *Auditing: Theory and Practice,* 2d. ed., rev. and enl. (New York: Ronald Press Co., 1917), 50.

2. Federal Reserve Board, *Verification of Financial Statements (Revised)* (Washington, DC., 1929), 1.

3. *Ibid.*

4. American Institute of Accountants, *Examination of Financial Statements by Independent Public Accountants* (New York: AIA, 1936), 1.

5. *Ibid*, 8.

6. American Institute of Accountants. "Extensions of Auditing Procedure," *Journal of Accountancy 68* (December 1939): 379.

7. Securities and Exchange Commission. Regulation S-X, *Form and Content of Financial Statements* (Washington, D.C.: U.S. Government Printing Office, 1941, as amended to and including February 5, 1941), 3.

8. *Ibid.*

9. American Institute of Accountants. *Tentative Statement of Auditing Standards--Their Generally Accepted Significance* and *Scope* (New York: AIA, 1947), 11.

10. AICPA, Statement on Auditing Standards 1, *Codification of Auditing Standards and Procedures* (New York: AICPA, 1973), Appendix A.

11. American Institute of Accountants, *Internal Control: Elements of a Coordinated System and Its Importance to Management and the Independent Public Accountant* (New York: AIA, 1949), 5.

12. *Ibid*, ¶6.

13. AICPA, Statement on Auditing Procedure 49, *Report on Internal Control* (New York: AICPA, 1971).

14. AICPA, Statement on Auditing Procedure 52, *Reports on Internal Control Based on Criteria Established by Governmental Agencies* (New York: AICPA, 1972), ¶1.

15. *Ibid*, ¶50.

16. *Ibid*, ¶60.

17. *Ibid*, ¶65.

18. AICPA, Statement on Auditing Procedure 54, ¶70.

19. *Ibid*.

20. AICPA, Statement on Auditing Standards 9, *The Effect of an Internal Audit Function on the Scope of the Independent Auditor's Examination* (New York: AICPA, 1975), ¶11.

21. AICPA, Statement on Auditing Procedure No. 30, *Reporting on Internal Accounting Control*, (New York: AICPA, 1980).

22. AICPA, Statement on Auditing Standards No. 39, *Audit Sampling*, (New York: AICPA, 1981).

23. *Ibid*, *Appendix*.

24. *Ibid*, ¶33.

25. *Ibid*, ¶34.

26. *Ibid*, ¶41-43.

27. AICPA, Statement on Auditing Standards No. 47, *Audit Risk and Materiality in Conducting an Audit*, (New York: AICPA, 1983).

28. AICPA, Standard on Auditing Standards No. 48, *The Effects of Computer Processing on the Audit of Financial Statements*, (New York: AICPA, 1984).

29. AICPA, Standard on Auditing Standards No. 55, *Consideration of the Internal Control Structure in a Financial Statement Audit*, (New York: AICPA, 1988).

30. *Ibid*, ¶08.

31. AICPA, Statement on Auditing Standards No. 60, *Communication of Internal Control Structure Related Matters Noted in an Audit*, (New York: AICPA, 1988).

32. AICPA, Statement on Auditing Standards No. 65, *The Auditor's Consideration of the Internal Audit Function in an Audit of Financial Statements*, (New York: AICPA, 1991).

33. COSO members include the American Institute of Certified Public Accountants (AICPA), the Financial Executives' Institute (FEI), the Institute of Internal Auditors (IIA), the Institute of Management Accountants (IMA), and the American Accounting Association (AAA).

34. *Internal Control—Integrated Framework*, Committee on Sponsoring Organizations of the Treadway Commission, (New York: COSO, 1992).

35. AICPA, Statement on Auditing Standards No. 78, *Consideration of Internal Control in a Financial Statement Audit: An Amendment to SAS No. 55*, (New York: AICPA, 1995).

36. *Ibid*, ¶07.

37. *Ibid*, ¶10.

38. *Ibid*, ¶11.

39. *Ibid*, ¶12.

40. *Ibid*, ¶19.

41. AICPA, Statement on Auditing Standards No. 80, *Amendment of Statement on Auditing Standards No. 31, Evidential Matter*, (New York: AICPA, 1996).

42. *Ibid*, ¶12.

CHAPTER 3

The Relationship of Internal Accounting Controls to the Audit Program

As indicated in chapter 2, internal accounting controls play an important role in the audit process. This chapter briefly considers the kinds of audit evidence that the auditor may consider and presents a more detailed description of a typical audit planning procedure. This description emphasizes the role of internal accounting control evaluation in the design of an audit program.

The objective of an audit is to render an opinion on (1) the fairness of presentation, in conformity with generally accepted accounting principles, of results of operations for a given period of time and (2) the fairness of presentation of the financial position at the end of that given time period. To develop such an opinion, the auditor must gather and evaluate many different types of information, both financial and nonfinancial. It is the gathering and evaluation activity that is known as the audit process.

MANAGEMENT ASSERTIONS

Although preferability may have shifted over the years from one type of information, or audit evidence, to another, the basic audit process has undergone few major changes. It has emphasized gathering and evaluating evidence to judge five broad categories of management's assertions made in the financial statements. These five categories are:

1. That assets or liabilities of the entity exist at a given date and that income and expense transactions have occurred.
2. That all transactions and accounts that should be reflected in the financial statements are reflected in the statements.
3. That assets are the rights of the entity and liabilities are the obligations of an entity at a given date.
4. That all assets, liabilities, revenue, and expense elements have been properly reflected in the financial statements at appropriate amounts.
5. That particular elements of the financial statements are properly classified, described, and disclosed.[1]

When designing an audit program to obtain evidence to test these assertions, three factors affect the auditor's judgment (see figure 3.1). The first factor is the selection of procedures to obtain evidence from the various types of audit evidence available to the auditor. Governing this factor are two others — the need to satisfy generally accepted auditing standards and the auditor's personal criteria for accepting responsibility for the expression of an opinion.

TYPES OF AUDIT EVIDENCE

Audit evidence can be classified according to several characteristics, one of which is reliability. For example, audit evidence resulting from physical examination procedures is highly reliable to determine existence—but not ownership. In fact, physical examination of inventories is virtually required by generally accepted auditing standards. Relatively less reliable audit evidence results from a secondary category of audit procedures: confirmation with independent, outside entities. Although this evidence may not be as reliable as physical examination, confirmations are important enough to be virtually required by generally accepted auditing standards for receivables.

Evidence gathered by examining records maintained within the reporting entity is relatively less reliable. The results of this type of procedure are usually projected in financial terms to an entire population and then compared to the financial statement amounts in question.

Physical examination, confirmation procedures, and examination of records are referred to as substantive tests.

Figure 3.1
Factors Influencing the Designing of an Audit Program

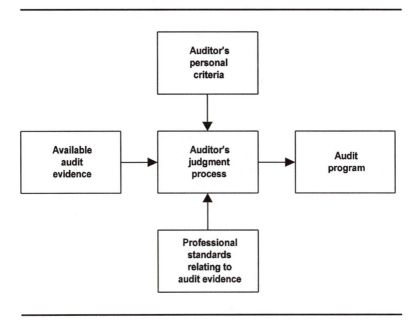

The other category of procedures consists of compliance tests, which are tests of compliance with the system of internal accounting control procedures. Compliance tests are performed after the auditor has gained an understanding of the internal accounting control system, and they are intended to estimate the inherent deviation rate within an accounting system. Under generally accepted auditing standards the auditors may not place complete reliance on internal accounting controls to the exclusion of other auditing procedures with respect to material amounts in the financial statements. This does not mean that compliance procedures are not important or should be avoided if possible. Since compliance tests are often less costly than substantive tests, they can reduce the cost of an audit.

The ability to substitute one type of audit evidence for another, however, can also create significant problems for the auditor. In determining a proper mix of procedures that would produce audit evidence of appropriate reliability, the auditor must make several subjective judgments. The auditor must determine, first, the potential reliance that may be placed on the system of internal accounting controls; next, the acceptable reduction of related substantive audit procedures; and finally, whether reliance would be cost beneficial.

PERFORMING THE AUDIT

To encourage a consistent approach to this judgment process, most auditors have developed some type of sequential decision system in which each judgment builds on the results of previously performed procedures. An example of such an approach, as it relates to the degree of reliance judgment in a particular audit area, follows.

1. Consider the internal control environment.

In developing an audit program, the auditor first obtains information on the environment in which internal accounting controls operate. The auditor considers if compliance with internal accounting controls is encouraged by management and if the circumstances appear to be conducive to the production of accurate and reliable accounting information.

One possibility of which the auditor must be aware is the deliberate circumvention of controls by management personnel, commonly termed "management override." Although it is usually impossible to determine with certainty those cases in which management has overridden the internal accounting controls, generally it should be possible to evaluate this risk. The evaluation may consider such factors as the type of organization being audited, the susceptibility of the area being examined to misstatement, the requirement for management judgment in determining the amounts in the records, and prior experience in auditing the entity's financial statements. Such an evaluation is not intended to assess the probability that management is overriding the internal accounting controls, but merely to assess whether the area being examined presents any significant potential for override.[2]

If the evaluation indicates a significant potential for management override, reliance on the internal accounting controls generally would not be appropriate. In those instances, substantive procedures should not be restricted.

2. Select audit procedures assuming no reliance on internal accounting controls.

The auditor should select substantive procedures from which reasonable assurance would be gained to meet specified audit objectives. The nature, extent, and timing of such procedures should be based on *no* reliance on internal accounting controls. An integral part of selecting substantive audit procedures is to consider the types of errors and irregularities that could occur. Once that has been done, the auditor can then select those substantive audit procedures that would be effective in identifying and evaluating the impact of each type of error or irregularity. A substantive audit procedure may be effective in identifying some types of errors or irregularities, but ineffective in identifying other types. For example, a particular substantive procedure may be successful in identifying mathematical mistakes but useless in identifying cutoff errors. Also, some procedures may be effective for overstatement errors but not for understatements.

3. Identity relevant internal accounting controls.

Internal accounting controls relevant to the reliance decision may be defined as those that are intended to prevent or detect the same types of irregularities or errors that related substantive audit procedures would be designed to detect. If such relevant accounting controls exist and are functioning as designed, the auditor can consider relying on those controls for purposes of changing the nature, extent, or timing of the substantive audit procedures. If no relevant accounting controls exist, the auditor should perform the audit procedures selected in step 2 or equivalent substantive procedures. Approaches to the identification of relevant internal accounting controls are discussed in chapter 4.

4. Select procedures that test the functioning of relevant internal accounting controls.

To determine if reliance on an internal accounting control is justified, the auditor must gain assurance that the control is functioning effectively and consistently. This is accomplished through the use of compliance tests. Such tests generate evidence of the likelihood that the control will fail to detect a specific error type. The design of the compliance tests should reflect the criteria by which an internal accounting control is to be judged. These criteria will reflect the auditor's judgment in regard to the expected degree of reliance that may be placed on the control. A simplified example showing one possible set of criteria is shown in figure 3.2.

Figure 3.2
Possible Relationship Between Control Reliability and
Extent of Reliance on Internal Accounting Control

Evaluation of Accounting Control Reliability	Situation	Expected Degree of Reliance
Good	Little likelihood of errors occurring or not being detected by control	Substantial
Fair	Some likelihood of errors or ineffective control	Some
Poor	Strong likelihood of errors or ineffective control	None

In choosing to test an internal accounting control for possible reliance, the auditor should keep in mind that there is always a possibility that the criteria established for expected degree of reliance will not be met. That is, the auditor may expect that compliance test results will indicate that "substantial" reliance is justified; however, when compliance tests are completed, only "some" or "none" may appear justified. In those instances, the auditor would be unable to reduce related substantive procedures to the extent anticipated. In choosing to test compliance, then, the auditor should expect a fairly high probability of success in achieving the established criteria.

A compliance test can take many forms. In fact, many audit procedures may be used as either a compliance test, as a substantive test, or both, depending on how the results of the test are interpreted. Indeed, the distinction between compliance tests and substantive tests is not definitive. In general, however, a compliance test is performed to evaluate the effectiveness of an accounting control in preventing or detecting errors; a substantive test, on the other hand, is performed to gain evidence about the accuracy of the financial information contained in the financial statements.

Compliance tests may consist of procedures as simple as observation and inquiry of client personnel. More complex procedures include performance of selected operations or independent calculations by the auditor. Techniques using statistical or computer-assisted analysis are also common.

5. Select audit procedures to be performed if the expected degree of reliance on internal accounting control is justified.

Auditing standards are broad requirements that allow the auditor the choice of several alternative methods of accumulating audit evidence. However, no alternative may be chosen if it fails to meet the sufficiency and competence criteria in the third standard of field work. Accordingly, even though one possible alternative was established in step 2, other alternatives that would provide equally sufficient and competent evidence may be selected. Typically, these other alternatives are based on reduced substantive procedures combined with successful compliance tests of internal accounting controls.

6. Perform cost analysis.

Professional standards recognize that an auditor typically has economic limits that must be met. Accordingly, if alternative sources of audit evidence, each equally sufficient and competent, are available, the auditor may select the source or sources that are most economical.

To accomplish this, the auditor must estimate the comparative costs of performing steps 7 and 8 (compliance tests combined with restricted audit procedures) and of performing step 9 (audit procedures reflecting no reliance on internal accounting controls).[3]

7. Perform and evaluate tests of compliance.

After the compliance tests have been completed, the results must be analyzed to determine the possible effects on related substantive audit procedures. If results indicate internal accounting control reliability is as expected, reduced substantive audit procedures may be appropriate. If results are not as expected, however, the auditor must evaluate the reliability of the accounting system and make appropriate adjustments to the substantive audit procedures. As before, such adjustments would be based primarily on professional judgment.

8. Perform and evaluate restricted substantive audit procedures.

In evaluating the results of restricted substantive audit procedures, any errors or exceptions that are noted should be evaluated by two standards:

    a. What is the potential impact of any monetary error when projected to the financial statements as a whole?

    b. What internal accounting controls must have failed to allow the error to occur and/or go undetected? How does this

information affect the auditor's previous evaluation of
internal accounting controls?

Errors found by substantive procedures may provide evidence that the
compliance tests did not project an accurate estimate of internal
accounting control reliability. Having found such conditions, the auditor
should immediately consider the effect on the overall audit plan, and he
should expand the scope of audit work in order to evaluate the nature and
extent of the problem and its effect on the financial statements.

9. Perform and evaluate substantive audit procedures.

If, at any point during the audit, it is determined that reliance on internal
accounting controls is not appropriate or not cost beneficial, substantive
audit procedures reflecting no reliance on controls should be performed.
The objective of such tests is to develop evidence in regard to the fairness
of presentation of the financial statements, and such tests are not intended
to result in conclusions about the reliability of the internal accounting
controls.

SUMMARY

This chapter has shown that different types of audit evidence may be used
by the auditor to test five basic assertions made by management
concerning the financial statements. In audit planning three factors are
important: (1) the auditor's personal criteria, (2) professional standards,
and (3) available audit evidence. These three factors allow the auditor to
select various alternative combinations of procedures. The selection and
implementation of those procedures were summarized in a nine-step
illustration. Of critical importance to the monograph are the steps dealing
with internal accounting control evaluation. Evaluation approaches are
discussed in chapter 4.

NOTES

1. AICPA, Statement on Auditing Standards 31, *Evidential Matter* (New York: AICPA, 1980), 3-8.

2. Robert K. Elliot and John R. Rogers, "Relating Statistical Sampling to Audit Objectives," *Journal of Accountancy* 134 (July 1972): 49.

3. The issue of cost analysis is discussed in greater detail in Jerry L. Turner and Theodore J. Mock, "Economic Considerations in Designing Audit Programs," *Journal of Accountancy* 149 (March 1980): 65-74.

CHAPTER 4

Approaches to the Evaluation of Internal Accounting Controls

Because of the lack of formal guidelines for evaluating internal accounting controls, many alternative approaches have been developed over the years. This chapter examines some of these approaches.

IDENTIFYING AND DOCUMENTING RELEVANT INTERNAL ACCOUNTING CONTROLS

The first problem encountered by the auditor is that of identifying and documenting the relevant internal accounting controls (defined in chapter 3). Traditionally, auditors have identified relevant internal accounting controls by observation and inquiry. Of primary concern are the safeguarding of assets and the clerical accuracy of the accounting records. The results of the observation and inquiry activities are usually documented in narratives in the workpapers. Although fairly easy to complete, such narrative documentation provides minimal aid for the auditor in identifying internal accounting controls. Accordingly, new methods have been developed to provide the auditor with some guidance.

As companies grow more complex, the corresponding review of internal controls becomes more cumbersome. To handle large and cumbersome reviews, extensive standardized internal control questionnaires have been developed. An example of a typical internal control questionnaire page is shown in figure 4.1. For a given account, the questionnaire generally lists all internal controls that might be relevant either to management or to an auditor. The lists are almost always in

Figure 4.1
Commercial Questionnaire on Internal Control
Accounts Receivable

Accountant		
Date		

Company_____   Period ended_____

Branch, division, or subsidiary_____

Question	Yes	No	Remarks
			Answer
Accounts Receivable			
1. Are accounts receivable ledgers balanced with general ledger controls monthly?			
2. Are monthly statements sent to all debtors?			
3. If there is more than one bookkeeper, are the bookkeepers assigned to different ledgers periodically?			
4. At least periodically on a surprise basis, do persons who are independent of the accounts receivable bookkeepers and billing clerks and who have no access to cash receipts:			
a. Compare monthly statements with trial balances, balance the statements with the general ledger control, mail the statements and investigate all differences reported?			
b. Compare trial balances and agings to ledgers?			
5. Are accounts confirmed periodically on a surprise basis by internal auditors or other independent officials?			
6. Are all claims for freight damage, shortages, unsatisfactory merchandise, etc., set up on the books or otherwise controlled as soon as the claims are prepared for filing?			
7. Are shipments on consignment, on approval, etc., handled separately from sales and excluded from the accounts receivable ledger?			

question form, with a "yes" answer indicating existence of that particular internal control and a "no" answer indicating lack of the control. The widespread acceptance of this form of evaluation is indicated in *Montgomery's Auditing:*

> The authors believe that a practical and useful device for investigating and recording the auditor's inquiries into the system of internal control is the standard questionnaire, prepared in advance for the use of staff members. Such a questionnaire, prepared by persons fully conversant with the problems of internal control, makes available to the staff auditor a large fund of accumulated experience, and furnishes a standard of comparison to measure the performance of the particular system under review.[1]

Although still used by many auditors, questionnaires tend to become more and more comprehensive and therefore more tedious to complete. The corresponding costs related to this type of evaluation tend to escalate as more and more questions are added, with few being deleted. Also, a major weakness of internal control questionnaires is the difficulty of relating the findings to the design of the audit program. When the auditor is faced with possibly several thousand questions, the effort required to identify the relevant controls becomes massive. Attempts have been made to assign subjective values to each question, indicating relative importance,[2] but this approach has had little success.

In an attempt to alleviate this problem, many auditors have turned to the use of flowcharts of the accounting system under review. A flowchart is a symbolic, diagrammatic representation of the accounting documents and their sequential flow in the organization. A flowchart may show the origin of each document and record in the system, the subsequent processing, and the final disposition of any document or record. In addition, it is possible for a flowchart to show the separation of duties, authorization, approvals, and internal verifications that take place within the system.[3] Although the flowcharts can become quite cumbersome and expensive to prepare, they have the advantage of allowing a more effective tie between the study of the internal accounting control system and the audit program. The flowcharts used in the field study are in Appendix A.

A currently evolving concept involves the use of the computer to aid in identifying and evaluating internal accounting controls. The computer can be used to store abstract representations of an internal control system. These representations can be used to identify the existence, or the lack, of relevant internal accounting controls. Because of the computer's capabilities, highly complex analyses can be performed that could not be done without computer assistance. An example of the use of computers to document a control system is TICOM, developed by Cash, Bailey, and Whinston.[4]

AIDS TO ANALYSIS

An important step in the evaluation of internal accounting controls is the preparation of some form of organizing workpaper. Such a workpaper relates the relevant internal accounting control strengths and weaknesses to the audit procedures to be applied to the area being examined. One type of organizing workpaper is the "bridging" workpaper, such as the one used in the field study in Appendix A. This bridging workpaper documents the audit objective, the internal control strengths and weaknesses, the audit implications of those strengths and weaknesses, and the audit procedures selected to achieve the audit objective.

A different form of organizing workpaper is shown in figure 4.2. This workpaper is designed around transaction error types. In addition, some information about reliance to be placed on internal accounting controls is included, as well as the potential effect that each error type might have on the financial statements,

Many other types of organizing workpapers have been devised, emphasizing different aspects of the relationship between internal accounting controls and audit procedures. Regardless of form, however, all have the same basic purpose: to aid the auditor in making decisions about the extent of reliance to place on the system of controls.

METHODS OF EVALUATING INTERNAL
ACCOUNTING CONTROLS

As already noted, the auditor may choose from several alternative sets of audit procedures, each of which would satisfy both the auditor's personal criteria and generally accepted auditing standards. Typically, among the various alternative sets of procedures, one set of substantive procedures reflects no reliance on internal accounting controls, and the other sets are based on various reductions in substantive procedures combined with successful tests of compliance of internal accounting controls. A primary problem for the auditor is to determine that each alternative set of procedures considered produces equally sufficient and competent audit evidence.

The problem of determining equal sufficiency and competence can be approached with or without a formal model. The approach without a formal model requires that the auditor design and adjust the nature, extent, and timing of combinations of audit procedures until an indifference point, based on the auditor's judgment, is reached about which combination of procedures should be performed. In doing this, the auditor actually is using professional judgment to adjust the audit risk inherent in each combination of procedures to a perceived level of equal sufficiency and competence. Such a judgmental approach has been the traditional method used to design audit programs and is still the most common practice.

In recent years, however, applications of modeling techniques to auditing have allowed the level of audit risk to be approached mathematically. This permits a direct mathematical comparison of alternative combinations of audit procedures. One mathematical approach to this concept is a probability statement to express the risk that after audit a material error still exists in the area of audit interest:

Figure 4.2
Organizing Workpaper

Transaction Error Types	Identified Controls	Maximum Possible Reliance	Weaknesses	Effect on Financial Statements						Compliance Tests		Substantive Tests	
				Cash	A/R	Allow D/Acct	Inv.	Net Sales	Costs Expenses	Procedures	Planned Reliance	Procedures	Planned Risk
SALES													
Made to unacceptable credit risk	A2 E1 E2 E3 E4	high				u			u	T1 T2	moderate	P4 P5 P7	moderate
Shipment unauthorized	A1 A2 B1	high				no effect				T1 T2	none	—	
Shipment inaccurate	A3	high			o/u		o/u	o/u	o/u	T1 T3	moderate	T18	moderate
Invoice not prepared	A1 B1	low	inadequate control over keypunch input		u			u		T1	none	T17 T18 T19 T6 T7 P6 P7	low
Invoice inaccurate	A3 B2 B3 B4 D2	high			o/u			o/u		T1 T3 T4	moderate	P1 P2 P9 P10	moderate
Invoice improperly recorded	B3 B4 D1 D2	high			o/u			o/u		T1	moderate	T20 T22 T24 T25 P1 P2 P7 P9 P10	moderate
CASH RECEIPTS													
Cash receipts not recorded	C1 C2 C3 C4 C5 D1	high		u	o					T1 T9	moderate	P1 P2 P6	moderate
Amount recorded incorrectly	D2	high		o/u	o/u					T11 T15	moderate	T10 T14 T15 T21 T22 T24 T25 P1 P2 P6	moderate
OTHER													
Journal entries not authorized	D1 D3 D4	moderate		o/u	o/u			o/u		T1 T12	moderate	T13 T23 T24 T25 P3 P9	moderate
Uncollectable accounts not written off	E4 E5	high			o	o				T1	low	T24 T25 P4 P5	low
Improper classification or inadequate disclosure											none	P3	low

1. Legend of Identified Controls
A1 Sales orders prenumbered and controlled
A2 Sales orders independently authorized or approved
A3 Quantities ordered, shipped, recorded are independently checked
B1 Sales order (see A1 and A2) is shipping order
B2 Price list maintained (computerized)
B3 Daily sales independently received
B4 Sales detail independently reconciled to accounts receivable
C1 Prelisting of cash receipts
C2 Remittance advance used and compared to checks received
C3 Deposit slip independently checked to cash receipts journal
C4 Receipts deposited intact daily
C5 Bank account reconciled monthly by independent person
D1 Detailed accounts receivable reconciled to control monthly
D2 Monthly statements sent to customer
D3 Credit memos require approval
D4 Returned goods require receiver
D5 Advanced to employees require authorization
E1 New customers require separate approval
E2 Sales orders matched against delinquent list and credit limits before
    processing
E3 Credit limits periodically reviewed
E4 Monthly aged trial balance prepared and delinquent accounts reviewed
E5 Bad debt write-offs require approval

2. o   Overstatement error
    u   Understatement error
    o/u   Over or understatement error

3. Legend of Tests and Procedures
T1 Observation and/or inquiry

For customer orders:
T2 Ascertain approval or authorization
T3 Ascertain initiality of customer order signifying agreeing quantities
    on orders, bills of lading, and daily sales report; check whether
    quantities agree
T4 Ascertain initialing of customer order signifying that price was
    compared to price list; check whether prices agree
T5 Trace to monthly statement, A/r trial balance and subsequent
    credit (if any)
T6 Scan file for gaps in numbers
T7 Review on-order file for evidence of orders shipped but not billed

For those paid:
T8 Trace deposit slip to bank statement
T9 Trace to listing of remittances and ascertain whether cash receipts clerk
    agreed check amount to remittance advice
T10 Determine credit to proper customer
T11 Examine noncash credits for proper approval

For credit memos:
T12 Ascertain proper support and authorization
T13 Verify prices and extensions

For suspense report items:
T14 Trace to cash accept/reject report
T15 Examine support
T16 Trace to application on A/R trial balance

For bills of lading:
T17 Trace to sales order in accounting
T18 Agree quantities to sales order
T19 Trace sales order to daily report; note delay from shipping date

    Test footings and postings:
T20 Daily sales report
T21 Cash accept/reject report
T22 Weekly suspense report
T23 Large, unusual journal entries
T24 Monthly statement run
T25 Aged trial balance

For accounts receivable:
P1 Request confirmation of the recorded amounts
P2 Analyze and test the account from the date of confirmation to the closing date
P3 Review classification and disclosure
P4 Test aging
P5 Test subsequent collections
P6 Test period cutoffs of sales and inventory
P7 Analyze and evaluate allowance for doubtful accounts
P8 Reconcile accounts receivable detail file to general ledger balances
P9 Reconcile total credit to sales to debit to accounts receivable
P10 Reconcile sales order volume to capabilities, capacities, etc.

Source: Donald M. Roberts, *Statistical Auditing* (New York: AICPA, 1978), pp. 166-67.

$$R = p(e) \times p(1 - c) \times p(1 - s) \qquad (4.1)$$

where: R =   the audit risk.

$p(e)$ =   the probability of occurrence of material error in the area of examination in the absence of any internal control.

$p(1 - c)$ =   the probability of the failure of the system of internal control to prevent or detect material error.

$p(1 - s)$ =   the probability of the failure of the audit procedures to detect material error.

By use of the foregoing probability statement, the auditor can establish an acceptable level of risk and then determine the various combinations of probabilities that may achieve that level of risk. One of the primary problems in this approach is the difficulty involved in quantifying the various components of the probability statement. A common method is to use statistical techniques to estimate certain probabilities and to control certain others. Donald M. Roberts provides a more detailed discussion of these techniques.[5]

Another approach to quantifying the probability that the internal control system will fail to prevent or detect material error ($p(1 - c)$ in the preceding equation) uses concepts from reliability engineering. This approach views an internal accounting control system as analogous to a system composed of various electronic or mechanical parts. It assumes that the system is composed of a number of related procedures, that each procedure or set of procedures operates predictably, and that its operation can be described in probabilistic terms. Given the design of the system and the probability of failure of each component within the system, the overall system reliability can be calculated.[6] For this purpose, reliability is defined as the probability that a process will be completed with no errors.[7]

This approach can be illustrated by a series of diagrams showing the relationship between tasks or processes and their related controls. The first diagram represents two steps in a sequential process, where the output from step 1 is used as the input to step 2.

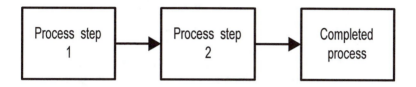

Reliability theory states that in a sequential process the overall reliability of the system is obtained by multiplying the individual component reliability estimates. For instance, if the reliabilities are 80 percent for process step 1 and 90 percent for process step 2, then the reliability of the completed process is 72 percent.

If the reliability of the output from a process step needs to be improved, some type of control can be added to evaluate such output. However, the addition of a control creates a greater complexity in the calculation of reliability. A typical control would consist of two components - the first, a signal to indicate whether the output was acceptable or unacceptable, and the second, some method of correcting unacceptable output. This is illustrated in the following diagram.

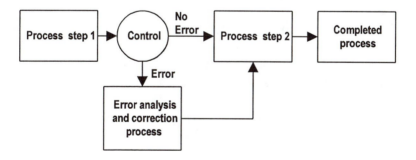

The complexity of the reliability calculation is increased as there are now three components potentially affecting the output of process step 1. For the input to process step 2 to have no errors, two of the three components must operate correctly. To model this situation, Barry E. Cushing identified the following parameters.

1. p = the probability that process step 1 is correctly executed prior to administering the control procedure.
2. $P(e)$ = the probability that the control step will detect and signal an error, given that one exists.
3. $P(s)$ = the probability that the control step will not signal an error, given that none exists.
4. $P(c)$ = the probability that the correction step will correct an error, given that one exists and has been signaled.
5. $P(d)$ = the probability that a failure of the control step will be detected and no correction made, given that the control signals an error when none exists.[8]

The relationships of these parameters are shown in figure 4.3. An examination of these relationships reveals that reliability would be the sum of the probabilities of the "successful," or correct, responses. This can be expressed as follows:[9]

$$R = pP(s) + p(1 - P(s))P(d) + (1 - pP)(e)P(c). \qquad (4.2)$$

Likewise, the probability of an error in the output of process step 1 would be the sum of the "failures" shown In figure 4.3.[10]

$$1 - R = (1 - p)(1 - P(e)) + (1 - p)P(e)(1 - P(c))$$
$$+ p(1 - P(s))(1 - P(d)). \qquad (4.3)$$

Figure 4.3
Relationship of Reliability Parameters

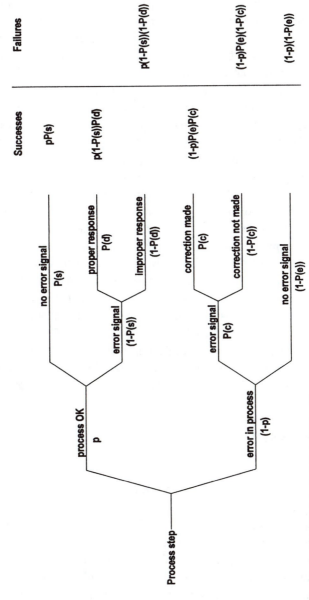

Source: Cushing, "Mathematical Approach", p. 28

These concepts can be expanded to encompass multiple error-multiple control situations and other variations in circumstances. In addition, concepts relating to feedforward mechanisms, human reliability, and cost analysis of control systems have been researched or suggested as research areas that may have some applications to reliability modeling.[11]

A different approach to internal control evaluation is the use of behavioral or sociometric techniques for analysis. This concept was first suggested by John J. Willingham in 1966 and was later researched by Douglas R. Carmichael and Robert J. Swieringa.[12] Sociometric techniques appear to be potentially useful, since the various definitions of internal accounting control have usually included "the plan of organization" as one of the elements. Expanding on this, Carmichael proposed that "the principal function of an internal control system is to influence (or control) human behavior."[13] Based on this idea, the study of the various relationships of the people involved within an organization may prove to be more relevant than the study of the tasks they perform. Several approaches in applying sociometric methods have been suggested.[14]

Reliability and sociometric methods have not been widely accepted in the auditing profession. Future research may find that combinations of the various proposed methods, or some new methods, will be more successful in analyzing and evaluating internal accounting controls. Until that time, however, the auditor's evaluation of internal accounting controls will continue to be made on the basis of professional judgment.

RELATING COMPLIANCE TESTS TO SUBSTANTIVE TESTS

Regardless of the method used to estimate the reliability of an internal accounting control system, the auditor must still evaluate the effect of such estimates on the need for substantive audit procedures. Because no accepted standards have been established, appropriate substantive audit procedures are selected on the basis of an auditor's professional judgment. Such judgment requires the auditor to make trade-offs between reliance on the accounting controls and reliance on substantive procedures. An example of three different control evaluations involving such trade-offs, each resulting in evidence subjectively judged to be equally sufficient and competent, is shown in figure 4.4.

It should be noted that even though circumstances indicate that "substantial" or "some" reliance may be appropriate, the auditor is not required to place such reliance. Accordingly, other combinations of procedures with equal or lesser planned reliance may be evaluated as alternatives, as long as each combination results in evidence judged to be equally sufficient and competent.

Figure 4.4
Three Different Control Evaluations With Corresponding Sets of Audit Procedures Resulting in Equally Sufficient and Competent Evidence

Control Evaluation	Good	Fair	Poor
Reliance	Substantial	Some	None
Compliance Tests			
Extent	Tight Precision	Loose Precision	None
Timing	Interim – Well before year-end	Interim – Near year-end	N/A
Substantive Tests			
Extent	Maximum Restriction	Some Restriction	No Restriction
Timing	Interim with interim to year-end review and testing required	Interim with interim to year-end review and testing required	Year-end

SUMMARY

This chapter has summarized some of the basic approaches to the identification, documentation, and evaluation of internal accounting controls. Because of various complexities and difficulties in applying some of these approaches, few have achieved wide acceptance, particularly with respect to evaluation of accounting controls. Current practice relies heavily on professional judgment in evaluating internal accounting controls and their effect on substantive audit procedures.

NOTES

1. R.H. Montgomery, N.J. Lenhart, and A.R. Jennings, *Montgomery's Auditing,* 7th ed. (New York: Ronald Press Co., 1949), p. 56.

2. R. Gene Brown, "Objective Internal Control Evaluation," *Journal of Accountancy* 114 (November 1962): 50-56.

3. Alvin A. Arens and James K. Loebbecke, *Auditing: An Integrated Approach* (Englewood Cliffs, N.J.: Prentice-Hall, 1976), p. 170.

4. James I.Cash, Jr., Andrew D. Bailey, Jr., and Andrew B. Whinston, "The TICOM Model--A Network Data Base Approach to Review and Evaluation of Internal Control Systems," *Proceedings of the American Federation of Information Processing Societies Conference* (Montvale, N.J.: AFIPS, 1977).

5. Donald M. Roberts, *Statistical Auditing* (New York: AICPA, 1978).

6. Michael J. Barrett, Donald W. Baker, and Donald E. Ricketts, "Internal Control Systems: How to Calculate Incremental Effectiveness and Cost Using Reliability Concepts," *Internal Auditor* (October 1977): 31-43.

7. Barry E. Cushing, "A Mathematical Approach to the Analysis and Design of Internal Control Systems," *Accounting Review* 49 (January 1974): 26.

8. *Ibid.*

9. *Ibid.*

10. *Ibid.*, p. 27.

11. See George Bodnar, "Reliability Modeling of Internal Control Systems," *Accounting Review* 50 (October 1975): 747-57, and Akira Ishikawa, "A Mathematical Approach to the Analysis and Design of Internal Control Systems: A Brief Comment," *Accounting Review* 50 (January 1975): 148-50.

12. John J. Willingham, "Internal Control Evaluation–A Behavioral Approach," *Internal Auditor* 23 (Summer 1966): 20-26; Douglas R. Carmichael, "Behavioral Hypotheses of Internal Control," *Accounting Review* 45 (April 1970): 235-45; and Robert J. Swieringa, "A Behavioral Approach to Internal Control Evaluation," *Internal Auditor* 29 (March/April 1972): 30-45.

13. Carmichael, "Behavioral Hypotheses," p. 235.

14. Robert J. Swieringa and Douglas R. Carmichael, "A Positional Analysis of Internal Control," *Journal of Accountancy* 131 (February 1971): 34-43, and Robert J. Swieringa, "An Inquiry into the Nature and Feasibility of a Sociometric Analysis of Internal Control" (Ph.D. diss., University of Illinois, 1969).

The Internal Accounting Control Experiments: Introduction and Task Description

Chapters 5 through 10 of this monograph discuss the underlying research questions, methodology, and results of a series of five interrelated experiments on internal accounting control evaluation. Chapter 5 introduces the research questions addressed and presents a detailed discussion of the basic experimental task. Chapter 6 considers existing professional and theoretical guidelines about how an auditor should address the audit planning task in an environment of improving internal accounting controls. General hypotheses are derived and potentially important behavioral factors are identified. In chapter 7 the research methods and design used in the internal accounting control experiments are detailed. The discussion of experimental results is contained in four chapters. Chapters 8 and 9 discuss the effects of a number of factors—internal accounting controls, audit planning aids and approaches, and demographics—on the auditor's recommended sample sizes. Chapter 10 contains a discussion of the effects of the various experimental treatments on the content of auditor rationale memos and Chapter 11 discusses the results of the protocol analysis. Also, a summary of a study used to investigate the auditor's decision process is presented. The final chapter summarizes the research and presents implications for the accounting profession.

GENERAL RESEARCH QUESTIONS

Previous chapters have described the complexity and the judgmental nature of the auditor's study and evaluation of internal accounting controls.

In the early stages of the research, attempts were made (1) to develop a means of modeling or depicting an auditor's judgment process and (2) to identify the judgments that an auditor usually would make while evaluating internal accounting controls. The first objective led to an "input-process-output" model, which is depicted in a simplified form in figure 5.1. The second objective resulted in an inventory (see figure 5.2) of judgments that may be required as the auditor plans and implements the portions of an audit program relating to internal accounting control evaluation. The model (figure 5.1) assists in the identification of the cues, information, and criteria that form the basis of an auditor's judgment. The requisite input can be quite extensive, even for the audit of a small entity. This will be evident when the case materials underlying the experiments are presented.

Figure 5.1
Simplified Judgment Model

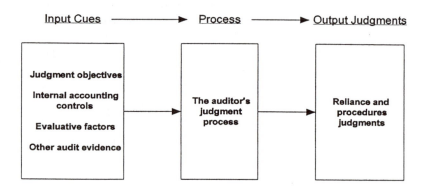

Figure 5.2, an inventory of reliance and procedure judgments relevant to internal accounting control evaluations, illustrates the complexity of the auditor's task. The figure includes eleven judgments, whereas the experimental study examines only the fourth procedure judgment: "How should reliance judgments affect the extent of substantive testing?" This judgment is of particular interest because it influences both audit efficiency and overall audit risk. Audit efficiency may be enhanced if overall audit resources are reduced by an appropriate mix of internal accounting control evaluation and substantive evidence. Overall audit risk is affected by the reliability of the information produced by the accounting system and the reliability of the substantive audit procedures. Although the fourth procedure judgment is the general research question on which the experimental phase is founded, the experiments actually facilitate research into many, more specific, issues.

Figure 5.2
Inventory of Reliance and Procedure Judgments Relevant to the Study and Evaluation of Internal Accounting Controls

Reliance Judgments

1. Is the environment in which controls operate conducive to effectively functioning internal accounting control?

2. If the environment is conducive to effectively functioning internal accounting controls, does the auditor choose to place reliance on such controls?

3. Do specific related internal accounting controls considered together provide reasonable assurance against the undetected occurrence of material errors or irregularities?

4. Do specific internal accounting controls that were compliance-tested provide reasonable assurance against the undetected occurrence of material errors or irregularities?

5. For areas where compliance test results were not satisfactory, are there other internal accounting controls on which reliance may be placed?

6. For reliance areas where the auditor has performed compliance tests up to an interim date, should compliance tests be extended to the remainder of the period being tested?

Procedure Judgments

1. What method of documentation of internal accounting controls would be appropriate?

2. What compliance tests would be most effective?

3. Can internal accounting controls identified in reliance judgment 5, above, be compliance-tested effectively? If so, what compliance tests would be appropriate?

4. How should reliance judgments affect the extent of substantive testing?

5. What types of tests would be appropriate for the period after interim?

A second area of general research interest arose as various auditor input-process-output decision models were developed. Specifically, were the judgment inputs contained in the models (for example, figure 5.1) and in the literature the actual inputs that the auditors considered and upon which they relied? By asking the experimental subjects (auditors) to document their logic in "rationale memos," experimental evidence was obtained.

PREVIOUS RESEARCH CONCERNED WITH THE EFFECT OF INTERNAL ACCOUNTING CONTROL RELIANCE ON AUDIT PROGRAMS

General references are presented in this section to help set the scope and to describe the nature of the research problems. Literature that bears more directly on tested hypotheses is contained in subsequent chapters.

Previous research on the auditor's study and evaluation of internal accounting controls may be classified as being either normative or descriptive. Normative research is also of two types—authoritative or optimal. The authoritative literature, discussed in earlier chapters, is important partly because it specifies decision inputs (cues and factors) that auditors should consider and document.

The second class of normative research, which derives from decision theory, has recently been applied to auditing.[1] This research has the goal of specifying an optimal audit decision, such as sample size, or mix of audit procedures.

A significant amount of behavioral and, in particular, human information processing research has recently appeared in accounting and auditing literature.[2] This research is primarily descriptive and involves the modeling of an auditor's judgment process in terms of available input cues used and their implicit weightings.

Descriptive research has also been conducted by use of field studies. For example, W. Morris and H. Anderson conducted a field study concerning the effects of the study and evaluation of internal controls on auditor extent judgments, with the following results: "Based on the audits included in the study, there exists no pervasive relationship between the auditor's evaluation of internal control and the amount of evidence obtained on the engagement."[3]

The descriptive research detailed in this monograph is based on controlled experimentation. The primary objective was to obtain empirical evidence on the effect of changes in internal accounting controls and differences in audit approach on auditor's sample size decisions. The experiments were designed to address both the general research questions discussed in the previous section and questions derived from previous research.

OVERVIEW OF THE EXPERIMENTAL
TASK AND AVAILABLE INPUT CUES

In the experiments, nearly 200 audit seniors and supervisors were presented a case containing information on improvements in internal accounting controls. They were asked to adjust, as they considered necessary, the planned sample size for four specific auditing procedures in an audit program. The experimental case study was based on a portion of a commercial entity's revenue cycle; it presented the subjects with nearly all the documentation normally available during an audit. A pilot study was conducted to verify the completeness of the data base. The documentation included consisted of the following:

1. The prior year's completed audit program and the current year's partially completed program.

2. A memo summarizing audit planning considerations (economic, organizational, management, general control environment, and other data).

3. Accounting system documentation (flowcharts).

4. "Bridging workpapers," which related audit objectives, system controls, compliance tests, and subsequent substantive procedures.

5. Results of interim compliance tests, which provided evidence of improvements in specific internal accounting controls.

6. Miscellaneous data, including interim financial information and results of the prior year's confirmation tests.

The subjects were informed that they were replacing an audit senior who had resigned during interim to take a position in industry and that they should perform the following tasks:

1. Evaluate the planned audit program for four procedures with respect to the extent of testing (see Appendix A for details):

   Procedure E-5:   Packing slip-invoice comparison.
   Procedure E-6b, c: Invoice pricing tests.
   Procedure E-9:   Posting test.
   Procedure E-10:   Confirmation of accounts receivable.

2. Prepare a memo for each procedure that summarizes their rationale for the audit manager's review.

As outlined above, this test situation provided data about the degree to which the subjects changed the planned sample size in response to year-to-year improvements in internal accounting controls. The experimental treatments were controlled by providing half the subjects with evidence of marked improvements in internal controls and the other half with fewer improvements.

For purposes of this discussion, the previous year's internal accounting controls are called "weak," those accounting controls that showed less improvement are called "fair," and the accounting controls that showed marked improvement are called "strong." These terms refer to the accounting controls as a group and do not always apply to each accounting control within the group. Details of specific accounting control changes are discussed in the next chapter.

The experimental task may be depicted as an input-process-output model, as is shown in figure 5.3. This figure organizes the available data, as was done previously in figure 5.1, and indicates the inputs and judgment requirements that differed among the five related experiments.

Examples and summaries of typical case materials actually used in the experiments are contained in Appendix A. The reader is encouraged

Figure 5.3

Judgment Model Depicting Experimental Task

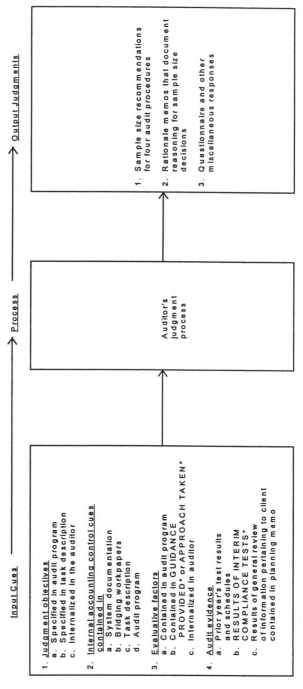

Input Cues → **Process** → **Output Judgments**

1. **Judgment objectives**
   a. Specified in audit program
   b. Specified in task description
   c. Internalized in the auditor

2. **Internal accounting control cues contained in**
   a. System documentation
   b. Bridging workpapers
   c. Task description
   d. Audit program

3. **Evaluative factors**
   a. Contained in audit program
   b. Contained in GUIDANCE PROVIDED* or APPROACH TAKEN*
   c. Internalized in auditor

4. **Audit evidence**
   a. Prior year's test results and schedules
   b. RESULTS OF INTERIM COMPLIANCE TESTS*
   c. Results of general review of information pertaining to client contained in planning memo

Auditor's judgment process

1. Sample size recommendations for four audit procedures

2. Rationale memos that document reasoning for sample size decisions

3. Questionnaire and other miscellaneous responses

*Capitalized items indicate the variables that differed, depending on which of the 5 versions of the experiment the subject performed.

to study these materials in detail to understand better the normative analysis of the case contained in the next chapter.

SUMMARY

Chapter 5 has explained several judgments that are important in the auditor's study and evaluation of internal accounting controls. The judgment relating changes in internal accounting controls to the extent of substantive audit procedures was selected for experimental study. Previous research was discussed, and an audit planning task that provided the basis for a series of five interrelated experiments was described.

The decisions required of the auditors who completed the planning task are complex. The next chapter contains a normative analysis of the task and develops research hypotheses.

NOTES

1. For a review of both normative and descriptive studies, see W. Thomas Lin, Theodore J. Mock, Lauren K. Newton, and Miklos A. Vasarhelyi, "A Review of Audit Research," working paper, University of Southern California, 1977.

2. For a comprehensive review of human information processing research, see Robert Libby and Barry L. Lewis, "Human Information Processing Research in Accounting: The State of the Art," *Accounting, Organizations, and Society,* vol. 2, no. 3 (1977): 245-68.

3. William Morris and Herschel Anderson, "Audit Scope Adjustments for Internal Control," *CPA Journal* 46 (July 1976): 15-20.

CHAPTER 6

Normative Analysis of the Audit Planning Task: Development of General Research Hypotheses

The Olde Oak audit case contained in Appendix A presented the experimental subjects with a complex and realistic audit planning problem. This chapter discusses alternative normative approaches that have been suggested in academic and professional literature and that may be applied to audit tasks concerned with the study and evaluation of internal accounting controls. A detailed analysis of Olde Oak is presented and hypotheses are derived about (1) how the improving internal accounting controls are expected to affect auditor decisions and (2) how several important behavioral variables may be expected to have an impact on these decisions. The final section of chapter 6 considers the subjects' second major experimental task: preparing a memo documenting their rationale. The norms for rationale memo content are discussed from the perspective of the audit review process.

ALTERNATIVE APPROACHES TO A NORMATIVE ANALYSIS OF AUDITOR'S EXTENT DECISIONS

Two general approaches to determining "appropriate" or "optimal" auditor sample size decisions pervade the appropriate literature. The first focuses on formal decision models. The second is based on professional standards, such as Statement on Auditing Standards 1, section 320, and expert consensus.

Formal Decision Model Approaches

Kinney attempted to integrate internal control evaluation and related judgments into a comprehensive decision model.[1] His approach is comprehensive in the sense that it jointly considers decisions concerning system design, internal controls, analytical review procedures, and detail tests. Two problems arise in applying this approach to Olde Oak: (1) It is difficult to measure certain needed variables, such as payoff and costs, and (2) the experimental task in Olde Oak is only a portion of Kinney's more comprehensive problem.

Another formal decision approach is based on statistical sampling concepts. This approach initially seemed promising with respect to two questions that were encountered in designing the experiments:

1. Could any type of standard be developed against which the experimental results could be evaluated?

2. What were the appropriate "anchors" to be provided in the planned audit program?

Further analysis indicated, however, that no logically comparable statistical standard could be developed. Although both statistical and judgmental samples are affected by numerous variables (including an estimate of audit materiality, the degree of reliance placed on internal accounting controls, the strength of other related tests, the dispersion of population values, and the frequency and magnitude of errors), nobody has devised a unique method of incorporating these variables into a sample. This will become clear when the results of the statistical version of the experiment are discussed. Briefly, in the statistical version, auditors recommended a wide variety of audit sample sizes even though each auditor was presented with an identical audit situation. As might be expected, this result was also observed in the experiment requiring judgmental samples. There are no accepted standards regarding how to incorporate all possible variables relevant to the sample size decision.

Two other formal decision model approaches were considered as possibilities for developing normative standards, and both were discarded.

Reliability analysis, as discussed in chapter 4, presents a possible way to evaluate internal control networks, but the necessary reliability data were not available.

Formal simulation, which was used by Burns and Loebbecke, presented a fourth possibility.[2] However, this would have required data, such as statistical distribution of sales invoices and accounts receivables, not normally available to subjects.

Each of these formal approaches provides opportunities for further research, but none provides the norms needed to hypothesize the experimental effects of the improving accounting controls in Olde Oak.

Professional Norms

As demonstrated in chapters 2, 3, and 4, professional standards provide the auditor with broad guidelines and permit great flexibility in the use of conclusions about an entity's accounting controls when formulating the audit program. Yet these standards, which are based on expert consensus, provide a decision structure (as in figure 3.2) and an inventory of relevant input cues (as in figure 5.3), which are the basis of a feasible, normative analysis of the case. The decision structure in figure 3.2 includes (1) an evaluation of the general control environment, (2) identification of errors, irregularities, and relevant controls, and (3) selection of the nature, extent, and timing of compliance tests. Such a process has been detailed many times.[3] Accordingly, figure 3.2 forms the basis of the following normative analysis of the experimental case.

A NORMATIVE ANALYSIS OF THE SAMPLE SIZE SELECTION TASK

An analysis of a problem such as the experimental case should begin with a specification of the objective or objectives that underlie the audit task. In completing the Olde Oak case, each subject was asked to evaluate only this year's *audit program* in regard to the nature, extent, and timing of procedures. Given this task, an auditor should consider objectives related to the obtaining of sufficient and competent audit evidence. These notions were discussed in detail in chapters 3 and 4.

The auditor would also need to consider the evidence and cues available at the time of the audit program evaluation. In the experimental case, the audit program evaluation took place during interim work after initial planning, general review, system documentation, and several compliance tests had been completed. Thus, available cues, summarized in figure 5.3, included all the data contained in the Olde Oak case, including a complete planning memo, prior year's audit program, the current year's planned program, and system documentation. For purposes of deriving a normative analysis of the experiment, and thus hypotheses, only those items that were experimentally controlled (that differed among different subjects) warrant explicit discussion. The cues and variables that were the same for all subjects would not be expected to be significant determinants of different audit program recommendations.

Relevant System Strengths and Compliance Test Results

In evaluating Olde Oak's internal accounting controls for possible reliance, an auditor would be expected to consider exposures and internal accounting controls that may reduce such exposures.[4] Accounting controls on which an auditor may potentially rely can be referred to as strengths. Lack of internal accounting controls or ineffective controls can be referred to as weaknesses. For the experimental task, relevant accounting controls, strengths, and weaknesses refer to those that, in an auditor's judgment, would affect the error rates in the financial data being audited.

In Olde Oak, eight strengths and three weaknesses are identified in the system flowcharts, and their nature and audit implications are listed in the bridging workpapers. An auditor would be expected to critically evaluate such papers for errors. For instance, an undocumented strength labeled US-1 in figure 6.1 was incorporated within the experimental case.

Figure 6.1 contains a list of those system strengths and compliance test results that were experimentally manipulated in the case. Thus, those auditors randomly assigned the "fair" treatment were given interim compliance test results listed in column 3, and those randomly assigned the "strong" case received the compliance test results listed in column 4. All subjects received the same data concerning the prior year's compliance tests (column 2). Thus, the main research question involves measuring the effect of the "fair" versus the "strong" controls on auditors' revised audit programs for the following four audit procedures:

Audit Program Step	Brief Description
E-5	Sales Invoice/Packing Slip Comparison
E-6b, c	Sales Invoice Price and Extension Test
E-9	Accounts Receivable Posting Test
E-10	Confirmation of Accounts Receivable

Figure 6.2 contains an analysis of these procedures in terms of possible test objectives, controls that might affect sample size if the auditor relies on them, relevant compliance test results, and several other factors. This normative analysis is the result of "expert consensus," since it benefits (1) from the experimenters' evaluation of the case, (2) from a review of several experienced audit managers and partners, and (3) from a critical review of the rationale memos of the first seventy-three subjects. On the other hand, the case is rich enough for many other credible analyses to be possible. The crucial column in figure 6.2 is the fourth one, which shows the accounting controls that are relevant to the four audit procedures.

DEVELOPMENT OF HYPOTHESES ABOUT THE EFFECT OF THE INTERNAL ACCOUNTING CONTROL TREATMENTS

The second standard of field work implies that the extent of substantive audit procedures is inversely related to the reliance placed on a system of internal accounting controls. Such reliance is directly related to the strength of that system of controls. Thus, the initial hypothesis with respect to the effect of improving internal accounting controls would be a decrease in the recommended sample sizes (extent) of the four procedures for both experimental treatments (fair and strong), with a larger decrease for strong controls than for fair controls.

Figure 6.1
System Strengths, Changes in Compliance Test Results, and the
Audit Manager's Initial Evaluation for the Two Experimental Treatments

(1) Documented System Strengths	(2) Last Year's Compliance Test Results	(3) This Year's Compliance Test Results Fair Treatment	(4) Strong Treatment
S-1 Prenumbered sales invoices are a. Prepared for all sales. b. Issued sequentially. c. Numerically accounted for.	Issued without regard to sequence	No exceptions found	No exceptions found
S-6 The sales invoice customer suspense file is reviewed monthly for unmatched invoices.	Not following up	Not following up	Immediate follow-up
S-7 An independent clerk checks the pricing of invoice, extensions, and footings.	(Weakness noted in management letter)	Test failed on 33rd item	No exceptions noted
S-8 The manager reviews monthly statements and attached invoices and spot checks some invoices to customer statements.	Limited review and follow-up	Limited review and follow-up	Detailed review and follow-up
Undocumented System Strengths			
US-1 The dispatcher maintains an independent numerical packing slip file.	Numerous sequence errors and a missing slip	Moderate number of exceptions	No exceptions noted
(The audit manager's initial evaluation of the control environment is contained in the task description.)	"No reliance"	"Some reliance"	"Significant reliance"

A refinement of the initial hypothesis may be made if one considers the relationship between specific controls and specific procedures. The primary evidence of improvements in internal accounting control was the year-to-year change in the compliance test results of *specific* accounting control strengths, as described in figure 6.1. Yet a subject may not decide to adjust sample size solely on the basis of an evaluation of the specific accounting control strength(s) related to an audit procedure. For example, evidence of improvements in specific, irrelevant accounting controls may lead to judgments about the general control environment, which may, in turn, influence sample size decisions. Such an influence may be called "halo effect."[5] To test whether subjects were influenced by halo effect, there was no year-to-year improvement in compliance test results for any specific accounting control relevant to the packing slip-invoice comparison (E-5). One may hypothesize that, for E-5, if subjects reduced sample sizes as a result of halo effects, subjects working with the strong accounting control treatment would mak e greater reductions in recommended sample sizes than those working with the fair accounting control situation.

The basic experimental situation was also used to develop some limited evidence about the influence of the previously planned sample sizes on the subject's determination of the appropriate sample size. The issue is raised by Loebbecke:

> Generally, in auditing, the first examination for a new client is the most objective one. More time is spent on learning activities, more attention is given to the objectives of corroboratory activities, and there is a greater sense of awareness and skepticism. *In subsequent examinations, however, even the best auditor is biased by the preconceptions formed by preceding efforts and findings.*[6]

One of Mautz and Sharaf's tentative postulates of auditing also provides a basis for anchoring behavior. Postulate 6 states, "in the absence of clear evidence to the contrary, what has held true in the past for the enterprise under examination will hold true in the future."[7] To the degree that a subject's decision is influenced by a planned or previous sample, the individual may be said to *anchor* to it. Given that the case contained both the prior year's and the current year's audit programs, subjects may be hypothesized to anchor on those that may have an effect on sample size recommendations.

Figure 6.2

Normative Analysis of the Researched Audit Procedures

Audit Procedure	Objective Of Test	Nature Of Test	Controls That Might Affect Sample Size*	Nature of Exposure	Cost/ Benefit Alternatives	Relevant Compliance Tests**	Influence Of Other Evidence
Step E-5: packing slip comparison	Test assignment of initial economic value	Dual purpose	None	Overstatement or understatement	Could select from invoices if S-4 is in effect (combine with E-6a, b and E-10)	E-4	Errors noted in prior year
Step E-6b, c: pricing test (Interpretation A)	Test assignment of initial economic value	Dual purpose	S-7	Overstatement or understatement	Could combine with E-5 and E-9	E-6a	Some errors noted in prior year
(Interpretation B)	Test control over assignment of initial economic value	Compliance	None	Failure of control	None	E-6a	None
Step E-9: posting test	Test posting accuracy	Dual purpose	S-1, S-6 possibly S-8	Understatement	Could combine with E-5 and E-6b, c	E-3, E-7, E-8	Exceptions noted in prior years
Step E-10: confirmations	Test validity Test valuation	Substantive	S-1, S-6 S-7, possibly S-8	Overstatement	Could add negative confirmations or restratify sample	E-3,E-6a,b, c, E-7, E-8	Results of E-5, E-6a, b, c

* See Figure 6.1.
** See Appendix A for details.

These, then, are the general research hypotheses concerned with the effect that differences in the internal accounting controls compliance test results have on auditors' sample size recommendations. Chapter 7 expands on these hypotheses to consider the effect that certain types of guidance and differing audit approaches have on such recommendations. First, however, a normative analysis of the subject's second major task should be considered.

NORMATIVE ANALYSIS OF THE
RATIONALE DOCUMENTATION TASK

In addition to analyzing the four audit procedures, the subjects were requested to prepare rationale memos for the engagement manager that included their specific recommendations and documented their reasoning and analysis. Two of the purposes of this phase of the research were to gain insight into the factors that the subjects considered important in internal control evaluation and to consider the adequacy and comprehensiveness of such memos as they might relate to the review process. The review process is an important component of an audit, but little research has focused on it.

The normative question of what kinds of rationale should be contained in the memos was a difficult one to address. Little formal guidance is available, but implicit guidelines are contained in the professional literature.

The approach in this study is based on formal content analysis.[8] By reviewing the authoritative literature and a sample of the rationale memos, an initial "dictionary" of relevant cue categories was derived. The initial set of categories consisted of the items contained in the column headings of figure 6.2. These were refined during content analyses of subsequent experiments, primarily by evaluating the reliability of the judges coding the memos and the completeness of the coding scheme. The final set of cue categories with which the comprehensiveness of individual auditor memos was evaluated appears in figure 6.3. A comprehensive rationale memo should contain explicit rationale on at least the first seven cue categories, or the reviewer may be left in doubt about undisclosed items.

Figure 6.3

The Set of Cue Categories Used in Content Analysis

1.   Test objective(s)
2.   Audit risk in account or item
3.   Referenced controls
4.   Compliance test results
5.   Reliance placed
6.   Nature of population
7.   Cost/benefit factors
8.   Other cues relied on
9.   Specification of alternative or complementary procedures
10.   Statistical reasoning
11.   Heuristic reasoning
12.   Evaluation of planned sample size

Note: Items 1 through 7 represent a comprehensive set for review purposes.

SUMMARY

This chapter has presented normative analyses of the auditor's sample size decisions for the experimental case and of the type of information that should be contained in the documented rationale. The normative sample size analysis was derived from professional judgment because no optimal solution was available. General hypotheses about the expected impact of the improved compliance test results and of possible behavioral factors were also presented. The next chapter discusses the research methods that were designed to address these issues.

NOTES

1. William R. Kinney, Jr., "Decision Theory Aspects of Internal Control System Design/Compliance and Substantive Tests," *Studies on Statistical Methodology in Auditing,* Supplement to vol. 13 of the *Journal of Accounting Research* (1975): 14-29.

2. David C. Burns and James K. Loebbecke, "Internal Control Evaluation: How the Computer Can Help," *Journal of Accountancy* 140 (August 1975): 60-70.

3. See, for example, Donald M. Roberts, *Statistical Auditing* (New York: AICPA, 1978), or William C. Mair, Donald R. Wood, and Keagle W. Davis, *Computer Control and Audit*, rev. ed. (Altamonte Springs, Fla.: Institute of Internal Auditors, 1973).

4. Exposures may be defined as the possible financial consequences of errors or irregularities.

5. "Halo effect" is defined in psychology as "the tendency in making an estimate . . . of one characteristic . . . to be influenced by another characteristic" (Horace B. English and Ava Champney English, *A Comprehensive Dictionary of Psychological and Psychoanalytical Terms* (New York: Longmans, Green & Co., 1958), p.236

6. James K. Loebbecke, "Discussant's Response to A Decision Theory View of Auditing." *Contemporary Auditing Problems,* ed. Howard F. Stettler (Lawrence, Ks.: University of Kansas Printing Service, 1974), p. 73 (emphasis added).

7. R. K. Mautz and Hussein A. Sharaf, *The Philosophy of Auditing* (Menasha, Wis.: American Accounting Association, 1961), p. 42

8. Ole R. Holsti, *Content Analysis for the Social Sciences and Humanities* (Reading, Mass.: Addison-Wesley Publishing Co., 1969)

CHAPTER 7

Research Methodology and Hypotheses

Based partly on the lack of clear and consistent results in previous research on internal accounting control evaluation, a series of field experiments was designed to address the kinds of questions discussed in chapter 6. Other issues that were researched include the effect that explicit guidance to auditors has on their decisions and the decision process auditors use to search through available evidence.

SUMMARY OF RESEARCH DESIGN

A number of possible research approaches for addressing such issues are available, including case studies, simulation modeling, and experimentation (the primary method used here). Some previous experimental auditing research is open to criticism for being unrealistic. For example, Ashton's internal control evaluation task required many more reliability judgments within a very short period of time than an auditor would normally encounter.[1] Other studies have been archival, and thus lacked experimental control.[2]

This research is based on a realistic audit experiment. The chosen case which is explained in chapter 5 and in Appendix A was based on an actual audit client and presented the experimental subjects (auditors) with nearly all the documentation normally available during an audit.

The experimental design involved assigning subjects to one of ten possible cases in which both changes in internal accounting controls and guidance or decision approach were systematically varied. Changes in accounting controls were detailed in figure 6.1 according to the system strengths identified on system flowcharts and experimental differences in interim compliance test results. Controls improved in both cases, but more so for the strong treatment than for the fair treatment. Because internal accounting controls are frequently improving because of suggestions made by the auditor, this was considered to be the most realistic experimental case.

The second experimental treatment involved providing guidance related to the task or, alternatively, specifying a variation in approach to the task. Guidance differed: In one situation none was provided, in a second situation a narrative summarizing professional literature was provided, and in a third a highly structured planning form was provided. Approach was varied by requiring some of the auditors to take a statistical approach and, for others, requiring a joint decision in which the senior's decisions were reviewed by an audit manager. Each of these five treatments also varied in terms of the internal accounting control dimension (fair or strong compliance test results). The entire two-by-five research design is summarized in figure 7.1, which also shows the number of subjects assigned to each of the ten cells.

Figure 7.1
Summary of Experimental Design and Number of Auditors Assigned to Each Treatment

Change in Internal Accounting Controls	Guidance Provided or Decision Approach				
	No Guidance	Narrative Guidance	Structured Guidance	Statistical Approach	Manager Review
Weak to fair	18	19	18	17	15 teams
Weak to strong	18	18	17	17	15 teams

Note: To achieve experimental realism, subjects were selected from a single audit firm. Because of differences in methods of documenting controls and other aspects, replication of the exact case in other audit firms is not possible.

The task was set up with approximately two hours to complete the judgments, rationale memo, and any questionnaires that were administered. A debriefing followed the case.

DETAILS ON VARIATIONS IN GUIDANCE AND DECISION APPROACH

The experiments were conducted in two phases, with the no-guidance and narrative-guidance experiments encompassing phase 1 and the other three experiments following in the indicated order. The formal investigation of guidance effects is appropriate because practicing auditors are continuously provided with guidance, such as training, audit manuals, and professional standards. Four types of explicit guidance were provided: (1) a written narrative that reviewed professional literature (primarily SAS 1, section 320), (2) a highly structured planning form, (3) a statistical approach based partly on formal statistical documentation, and (4) the guidance provided by formal manager review. In addition, a control group was provided with no explicit guidance. Each of these experimental conditions may result in effects on the subject's sample size recommendations and rationale memos. Such hypothesized effects will be discussed in the following section of this chapter.

No Guidance

Phase 1 of the research provided thirty-six subjects with no explicit guidance materials regarding the study and evaluation of internal accounting control. Thus, these auditors provide a control group against which to measure other guidance treatments. Except for differences in the internal control treatments, these auditors evaluated the case exactly as it is given in Appendix A.

Narrative Guidance

The narrative guidance provided to thirty-seven subjects was intended to review the major cues contained in the professional literature. In summary, it contained:

1. A discussion of the judgment to rely on internal accounting controls in terms of
    - Professional standards (SAS 1. section 320).
    - System or transaction cycle analysis.
    - Definition of reliance and nonreliance areas.
    - Factors to consider.
2. Definition of compliance and substantive tests.

3. Discussion of
    - Relationships between degrees of reliance and extent of substantive testing.
    - Factors to consider in making extent judgments.

4. Discussion of purposes of rationale memos.

Structured Guidance

An initial evaluation of the effects of the narrative guidance showed little effect either on the subject's recommended sample sizes or on the content of their rationale memos. The next step was to design a highly structured planning documentation form that integrated guidance and documentation. For each of the four evaluated audit procedures, subjects were required to indicate the following on a sample size documentation form (Appendix B):

1. The objective(s) of the audit procedure being analyzed.

2. The kind(s) of audit risk the procedure was designed to identify.

3. The range of sample sizes subjects were considering.

4. Materiality.

5. Relevant internal accounting control strengths.

6. Reliance being placed.

7. Nature of the population.

8. Other factors (cost/benefit, related audit procedures, and so forth).

In essence, this documentation form was designed to elicit judgments about relevant cue categories. The actual categories were derived partly from an initial analysis of the rationale memos and partly from literature sources.[3]

Statistical Approach

The initial phase of these experiments revealed a great deal of variation among auditors in terms of both their sample size recommendations and the content of their rationale memos. To measure the effect of a statistical approach, the experiment described in this section was implemented.

The rationale that a statistical approach may affect auditors' judgments is contained in a number of sources, including SAS 1, sections 320A and 320B, and Roberts, who comments

> Statistics has been defined as "a body of methods for making wise decisions in the face of uncertainty" . . .
>
> . . . The auditor can determine the *extent* of testing more objectively when using statistical sampling in tests of details rather than judgmental samples. That is not to say that statistical sampling replaces the auditor's judgment. Rather, statistical sampling allows the auditor to exercise judgment relative to the amount of sampling risk that can be borne and to express that sampling risk quantitatively. . . .
>
> . . . However, quantification merely makes explicit that which has always been implicit. . . .
>
> Using numbers to reflect professional judgment improves an auditor's ability to communicate examination results to others.[4]

Although one might take issue with several of these points,[5] the probability of significant experimental effects of a statistical version of the experiments is high. Thus, the statistical approach version of the case was designed and administered to thirty-five auditors during the second week of a statistical audit training course.

Experimental guidance and approach effects that differentiate the statistical approach from the other experiments can be summarized thus:

1. In-depth guidance regarding statistical considerations in the study and evaluation of internal accounting controls and

related audit procedures was contained in the course and in the eighty hours of advance preparation.[6]

2. Additional guidance was provided for the packing slip comparison and confirmation audit procedures in the form of a completed and approved form entitled "Request for Approval of Statistical Sampling Application."   In particular, the request form contained cues with respect to

- Audit objective of the test.
- Definition of population, sampling unit, and error.
- Estimated sampling units.
- Type of test (attribute or variables).
- Relation of the attribute test to substantive test work and the planned degree of reliance.
- Confidence level (reliability) and upper precision limit.
- Materiality and risk considerations.

The experimental case given to the statistical approach subjects was identical to that of the standard Olde Oak case, except for the addition of the aforementioned approval forms and a change in one planned audit procedure. The confirmation procedure was changed to require a statistical, dollar-unit sample. The planned statistical parameters for the confirmation procedure were the following:

- Materiality = 1% of book value
- Beta risk = .05
- Acceptable overstatement = 20% of materiality
- Alpha risk = .05

Subjects were expected to critically evaluate these parameters on the basis of the experimental case. They were permitted either to use a computer-based software package to determine sample size or to calculate sample size by hand. Most used the computer package. Their rationale for the sample sizes was to be documented in a rationale memo.

Manager Review

For a number of reasons that have been raised in organizational behavior and decision-analysis literature, individual auditor recommendations may differ from audit team decisions.[7] For example, it may be hypothesized that "group judgment is more accurate and consistent than individual judgment."[8]

To explore the effects of group decision-making on decisions relating to internal accounting control, a fifth version of these experiments was designed and implemented. This version involved a senior-manager team, thus adding a formal review element to the experiment. The audit senior and the manager were both given copies of the Olde Oak case identical to those given to the no-guidance subjects. The instructions and procedure for this experiment were identical to those of the no-guidance version, with the following exceptions:

1. The senior's initial recommendations and rationale memos were given to the manager, who, in isolation, documented any comments on a review form.

2. The senior-manager team then met and decided on their joint decisions. The disposition of any manager comments was also documented on the review form. In some cases, the senior's rationale memos were also updated.

The rationale memo data collected were all analyzed after this joint meeting. It was difficult to identify changes that may have been made in these memos as a result of discussion between the senior and manager.

In implementing the five experiments, slight differences in case materials were necessary. A comparison of the materials for each experiment is summarized in figure 7.2. This table also summarizes the materials used in a separate protocol study and a no-anchor pilot study.

THE PROTOCOL AND NO-ANCHOR PILOT EXPERIMENTS

In addition to the five main experiments detailed in the preceding section, two other experiments were conducted. A protocol study, which is detailed in chapter 11, investigated auditors' decision processes. A no-anchor pilot experiment was implemented to test potential anchoring effects on sample size decisions; a more detailed discussion is contained in chapters 8 and 9.

Figure 7.2
Comparison of Materials Provided or Collected for Each Experiment

Item	No Guidance	Narrative Guidance	Structured Guidance	Statistical Approach	Manager Review	Protocol Analysis	No-Anchor Pilot
1. Biographical Data Form	Standard*	Standard	Standard	Standard	Standard	Standard	Standard
2. Guidance provided	None	Narrative based on professional literature	Comprehensive, structured rationale memo	Statistical test approval form	None (manager review comments)	None	Review of firm guidance on judgmental samples
3. Case (task description)	Standard: task, role, selected audit results	Standard	Standard, except for slight task modification	Standard, except that task included review of statistical test approval form	Standard for senior, except review phase	Standard, except for verbalization instructions and practice session	Standard, except that less time was budgeted and no written rationale was required
4. Decision form/rationale memo	Standard	Standard	Comprehensive, programmed (structured)	Standard	Standard	Abbreviated	Abbreviated
5. Manager's review form	None	None	None	None	Standard	None	None

6.	Planning memo	Standard	Standard	Standard	Standard	Standard	Standard in audit binder	None
7.	Audit programs (revenue cycle)	Standard (this and last year's)	Standard	Standard	Standard, except for E-10 planned as statistical	Standard	Standard in audit binder	This year's program only with no anchors
8.	System flow-charts and bridging workpapers	Standard	Standard	Standard	Standard	Standard	Standard in audit binder	None
9.	Request for statistical procedure approval form	None	None	None	For E-6 and E-10	None	For E-6 only	None
10.	(Post-) Experiment questionnaire	Standard	Standard	None	None	None	Verbal protocol	None

* "Standard" refers to materials provided in the original no-guidance experiment contained in Appendix A

EXPERIMENTAL PROCEDURES AND
SUBJECT SELECTION

Subject Selection

The experiments were conducted at approximately twenty offices within the continental United States, plus a national training center. The offices were chosen to obtain a wide geographical dispersion contingent on economies of scale of at least five subjects or subject teams per replication. Similar experiments were run at approximately the same time-period to minimize possible interchange among offices. Subjects were chosen by each office according to our specifications (audit seniors or supervisors with some commercial experience) and availability. Some possibility of selection bias exists because the experimenters were representing the firm's executive office. As figure 7.1 shows, over 200 auditors participated.

Case Introduction

In most offices the entire experiment was conducted in a large conference room. Participants were informed beforehand that they were to participate in a case study and that they could bring, or have access to, usual audit manuals and authoritative literature.

The introduction phase included the following elements:

1. An introduction and brief backgrounds of the experimenters.

2. A brief description of the audit research activities of the experimenters and of the importance of the research project.

3. A random assignment of treatments to the subjects.

4. A review with the subjects of their materials, task, and time constraints, as described on pages 1 and 2 of the case

study. The standard time budget was 30 minutes each for review of case materials, analysis and decision, preparation of rationale memo, and completion of questionnaire (if any).

Case Review and Decisions

The auditors then worked on the case. The case materials were organized in the order in Appendix A.

Debriefing

The final phase for each experiment consisted of a fifteen-minute debriefing that covered the purpose of the research and experimental design. Subjects were also queried about problems they may have had and about the completeness of case materials. The vast majority of subjects found the case to be complete and to be an interesting experience.

Data Collected

As figure 7.2 shows, the experiments generated the following items:

1. Sample size recommendations for the four audit procedures for all subjects.

2. Rationale memos.

3. Explicit, documented judgments concerning certain underlying variables for the structured-guidance and statistical approach experiments.

4. Complete, tape-recorded verbal analyses of the entire task in the protocol study.

5. Biographical data on all subjects.

Major Research Hypotheses

The experiments generated much data and numerous hypotheses. As figure 7.1 shows, the underlying experimental design can be displayed in a two-by-five matrix with two internal accounting control treatments and five guidance/approach treatments, which will be referred to simply as guidance treatments. The primary experimental hypotheses thus relate to the expected effects (if any) of the treatments on subjects' sample size decisions and rationale memos. Hypotheses concerning the internal accounting control effects were developed in chapter 6. Although the following does not represent a comprehensive listing of all tested or testable hypotheses, it does summarize the major ones for the purposes of this monograph.

Hypotheses Concerning Sample Size Decisions

H1—*General Effect of Improving Internal Accounting Controls.* For both the fair and strong treatments, the improvement of specific controls relevant to the price test, the posting test, and the confirmation procedure are expected to result in reduced sample size recommendations.

H2—*Differential Effect of Strong Control Treatment.* For the price test, the posting test, and the confirmation procedure, recommended sample sizes of subjects receiving the strong internal control compliance test results are expected to be significantly smaller than those of subjects receiving the fair treatment.

H3—*Halo Effect.* For the packing slip comparison, the improvement in the general control environment is expected to result in significantly smaller sample size recommendations for subjects receiving the strong control treatment than those of subjects receiving the fair treatment.

H4—*Anchoring Effect.* In contrast with a control group receiving no planned sample sizes, subjects are expected to begin adjusting from the originally planned sample sizes. This should result in significant differences in sample size recommendations between the subjects and the control group.

H5—*General Guidance Effect on Mean Sample Sizes.* The various guidance treatments are not expected to have any significant effects on recommended sample sizes.

H6—*Guidance Effect on Variability of Sample Size Recommendations.* Narrative guidance, structured guidance, the statistical approach, and manager review are all expected to result in reduced variability in sample size recommendations.

Hypotheses Concerning Rationale Memo Content and Interaction Effects

H7—*Guidance Effects.* The content of rationale memos is expected to vary according to the type and explicitness of guidance provided.

H8—*Interaction Effects.* The internal accounting control and guidance treatments are not expected to have any explicit interaction effects on either sample sizes or rationale memos.

Statistical tests of these and other hypotheses are presented in chapters 8 and 9.

PILOT TESTS

Pilot tests were conducted on the standard case materials in two separate offices. The testing was designed to evaluate the realism of the case, the comprehensiveness of the experimental materials, time budgets, and other aspects. In both pilot tests, participants were interviewed, and many of their suggestions were incorporated in the case. In particular, the time budget was relaxed, and the task requirements were made more precise. Because of time considerations, taped, in-depth interviews were dropped from the original procedures.

EXPERIMENTAL LIMITATIONS

The experimental design involved several trade-offs and limitations. The first involved complications that were knowingly permitted in the experimental situation for the sake of establishing a realistic task environment. Subjects had access to decision-influencing information other than the improvements in specific internal accounting controls. The task environment enabled them to consider alternative test approaches and to decide to delete completely the audit test in question or to pursue the perceived audit objective by obtaining other types of audit evidence (for example, evidence from analytical review procedures, such as gross profit analysis).

A second limitation involved the possibility of a confounding variable. The instructions told the subjects to consider the audit manager's initial decision about degree of reliance. For fair controls, the manager's initial decision was to place some reliance on internal controls for purposes of designing this year's substantive tests. For strong controls, the audit manager's initial decision was to place significant reliance on those controls. Thus, observed differences in sample size recommendations may be a function of both differences in internal accounting control compliance test results and the manager's initial reliance decision. On the other hand, auditors should arrive at their own independent judgments concerning reliance on the specific controls that relate to the evaluated audit procedures. In fact, very few rationale memos included the manager's reliance decision as part of the subject's reasoning.

Subject selection for these studies was also a source of experimental limitation. They were selected from a single audit firm, and the possibility of firm effects exists. The possibility of a selection bias was mentioned earlier. On the other hand, the selected sample has a number of advantages, including homogeneity of training and experience.

The control group used to test the anchoring hypothesis also presents some difficulties in generalizing any significant differences. As figure 7.2 shows, available materials and time availability differed between the no-anchor and the experimental groups. Thus, the test of anchoring is a weak one.

Finally, one must consider the traditional weaknesses of experimental research methods in interpreting the experimental results. These include lack of complete realism (external validity) and the possibility of lack of motivation. The task was designed to minimize these effects.

SUMMARY

This chapter has presented the research design, experimental procedures, and major research hypotheses of this research. The research design is based on control of two factors: internal accounting control treatment (two levels) and the guidance provided to the subjects regarding their evaluation of internal accounting control (five levels). Experimental procedures entailed analysis of an audit case that provided data about sample size decisions and documentation of the subjects' decision rationales. Hypotheses were derived concerning the effects of the experimental treatments on sample size decisions and rationale memo content. Other hypotheses concerning behavioral factors were also derived. The statistical analyses of these hypotheses are discussed in the following two chapters.

NOTES

1. Robert H. Ashton, "An Experimental Study of Internal Control Judgments," *Journal of Accounting Research* 12 (Spring 1974): 143-57.

2. William Morris and Hershel Anderson, "Audit Scope Adjustments for Internal Control," *CPA Journal* 46 (July 1976): 15-20.

3. For example, see the approach in Donald M. Roberts, *Statistical Auditing* (New York: AICPA, 1978), which is reproduced in figure 4.2.

4. Roberts, *Statistical Auditing,* pp. 1-2.

5. For example, Chesley's results question the ability of auditors to communicate unambiguously in quantitative terms. G. Richard Chesley. "Procedures for the Communication of Uncertainty in Auditor's Working Papers," *Behavioral Experiments in Accounting II.* ed. Thomas J. Burns (Columbus: The Ohio State University. 1979): pp. 115-49.

6. Note, though, that internal control evaluation was only one of many topics covered.

7. See Hillel J. Einhorn, Robin M. Hogarth and Eric Klempner, "Quality of Group Judgment," *Psychological Bulletin 84* (January/February 1977): 158-72, and Robert Libby and Roger K. Blashfield. "Performance of a Composite as a Function of the Number of Judges," *Organizational Behavior* and *Human Performance* 21 (April 1978): 121-29.

8. E. Michael Bamber, *Expert Judgment in the Audit Team: Perception of Judgment Differences* (Unpublished working paper, the faculty of Accounting, The Ohio State University, January 1979), p. 6.

CHAPTER 8

Experimental Results: The Effect of Improving Internal Accounting Controls and Differences in Guidance and Approach on Auditors' Sample Size Decisions

The previous three chapters explain the internal control evaluation experiments. The results of these experiments are discussed in two chapters. This chapter statistically analyzes the auditor's sample size recommendations in terms of experimental variables that may be expected to affect these recommendations. The analyzed variables include the experimentally controlled treatments (results of compliance tests of improving internal accounting controls and differences in guidance or approach) and individual differences among auditors, such as in experience and training. Chapters 10 and 11 present the experimental results with respect to the rationale memos and a protocol study of several auditors' information-search and decision processes.

EFFECTS OF EXPERIMENTAL TREATMENTS ON SAMPLE SIZE RECOMMENDATIONS

Hypotheses concerning sample size recommendations were developed in chapter 7. The hypotheses may be classified into three areas: (1) experimental differences in average sample sizes (H1, H2, and H5), (2) experimental differences in the variability of sample size recommendations (H6), and (3) behavioral tendencies (H3 and H4). In general, these hypotheses predict differences (in some cases insignificant differences) in average sample sizes or in variability according to systematic differences in the experimentally controlled treatments.

Several conventions were used in analyzing the data. First, the following analyses of sample size decisions apply only to what are defined as valid subject decisions. Invalid decisions included (1) recommendations that did not specify an explicit sample size (for example, "I believe procedure E-5 should be reduced"), (2) recommendations that eliminated a particular audit step, and (3) decisions deemed invalid because the subjects did not complete the exercises satisfactorily (because they were interrupted with job requirements, because they misunderstood the task, or for other reasons). Only a few subject responses were eliminated as a result of the third criterion, but many responses were eliminated as a result of the first two, especially for the posting test (E-9). The second criterion was imposed because the experiments were designed primarily to investigate the effect that improving internal accounting controls has on auditors' reliance and sample size judgments. Professional standards do not permit total reliance on internal controls; thus, procedures that were eliminated through zero sample size recommendations were eliminated for other reasons.[1] Statistical analysis applied to the no-guidance and narrative-guidance experiments showed no significant difference in results if the second criterion was not imposed. The subjects' sample size recommendations are displayed in figures C.1, C.2, C.3, and C.4 in Appendix C.

The second convention that was applied to the data concerns the confirmation procedure (E-10). The planned audit program specified 439 positive confirmations, but the subjects were permitted to alter the planned program as they deemed necessary, and many auditors recommended negative confirmations or some combination of negative and positive confirmations.[2] Although positive and negative confirmations may not be equivalent in terms of information content, this study uses the aggregate number of confirmations in subsequent analyses of E-10.

EFFECT OF EXPERIMENTAL TREATMENTS
ON SAMPLE SIZES

Several of the major hypotheses that were derived from the normative analysis in chapter 6 and that were stated in chapter 7 deal with the effect of the controlled, experimental treatments on sample size recommendations. Figures 8.1 and 8.2 present the basic results that are relevant to these hypotheses. Figure 8.1 contains, for each of the four audit procedures, (1) the sample size recommendations that were contained in the planned audit program (row 1), (2) the average sample size, standard deviation, range, and coefficient of variation measured over all valid subject responses (rows 2, 3, 4, and 5), (3) average sample sizes for subjects receiving evidence of fair and strong accounting controls (rows 6 and 7) and (4) average sample sizes for subjects working under the various guidance treatments (rows 8 through 13). The figure shows the manager review results for both the joint manager-senior decision and the senior's decision prior to manager review, although only the joint decisions are used in the subsequent analyses. In figure 8.2 the results are further broken down to show the results for the entire two-by-five research design.

Hypothesis H1 predicted that, given the improvement in compliance test results over the prior year for both the fair and strong treatments, reduced sample sizes could be expected.[3] A comparison of rows 1 and 2 in figure 8.1 shows that averages over all subjects support hypothesis H1. But considering the effects of the internal accounting control treatments (rows 6 and 7), only for the strong treatment was there a consistent reduction over all procedures. No statistical tests were run for H1 because a difference between planned and overall average sample sizes may result from factors other than internal accounting control differences, such as substitution of alternative procedures.[4] Statistical analysis of the experimental effects of the treatments are presented in the analysis of variance (ANOVA) data in figures 8.3 and 8.4.

In figure 8.3 one-way ANOVA is used to investigate whether a statistically significant amount of the variance in auditors' sample size recommendations can be explained using a one-way classification of fair versus strong internal accounting control treatment. Recall that hypothesis

H2 predicted significant internal accounting control differences in sample sizes for the price, posting, and confirmation audit procedures. Figure 8.3 shows mixed results. Over all experiments, sample size recommendations are significantly different (actually smaller: See figure 8.2) for subjects receiving strong as opposed to fair controls. Yet, analysis of the results by guidance treatment show that the effect for the pricing, posting, and confirmation procedures is significant in only seven of fifteen cases.[5] In twelve of the fifteen cases, however, the average sample size difference was in the expected direction. Overall, these one-way ANOVAs support the notion that the subjects were systematically reducing sample sizes more given the comparatively better compliance test results for the strong internal accounting control treatment.

These results are also verified in the two-way ANOVAs contained in figure 8.4 which statistically accounts for both the internal accounting control and guidance treatments plus any possible interaction effects. In all cases, the internal accounting control effects are statistically significant and in the expected directions. Also, contrary to hypothesis H5, guidance effects are significant for three of the four audit procedures. The data in figure 8.1 suggest that guidance differences are primarily a result of the larger sample size recommendations for the statistical approach experiment. Figure 8.4 also indicates that there was no significant interaction effect between the two treatments, as hypothesized in H8.

EFFECT OF EXPERIMENTAL TREATMENTS ON THE VARIABILITY OF SAMPLE SIZE RECOMMENDATIONS

Variability in professional judgment is an issue that has attracted the interest of researchers in psychology for many years and that more recently has attracted the attention of researchers in auditing. With respect to variability in auditor extent decisions, a wide range in recommended sample sizes increases the likelihood of unwarranted reliance on small samples. For samples at the large end of the range of recommendations, the risk is one of overauditing. Of course, sample size is not the only factor to consider in evaluating such risks. Because the auditor has flexibility in program design, analysis of the entire mix of audit procedures would be necessary to determine audit risk.

Figure 8.1
Average Sample Sizes Classified by Experimental Treatment
(Averaged over all valid subject responses within each category)

	E-5 Packing Slip Comparison	E-6 Pricing Test	E-9 Posting Test	E-10 Confirmations
1 Planned sample sizes	150	75	100	439
Overall experimental results:				
2 Average sample size	88	69	81	381
3 Standard deviation	62.4	36	62.6	173.6
4 Range	390	290	382	854
5 Coefficient of variation	0.71	0.52	0.77	0.46
6 Fair controls	98	80	94	424
7 Strong controls	79	59	68	337
8 No guidance	79	73	65	351
9 Narrative guidance	85	72	66	364
10 Structured guidance	82	58	75	354
11 Statistical approach	125	77	126	531
12 Manager review				
Joint	76	66	78	321
Senior	74	53	68	368

Figure 8.2
Descriptive Statistics for Subjects' Sample Size Decisions
for the Four Evaluated Audit Procedures

Experiment		Packing Slip Comparison				Pricing Test				Posting Test				Confirmation Procedure			
		Mean	Std. Dev.	Coef. of Var.	Range	Mean	Std. Dev.	Coef. of Var.	Range	Mean	Std. Dev.	Coef. of Var.	Range	Mean	Std. Dev.	Coef. of Var.	Range
No guidance	Fair	94	56	0.60	175	84	40	0.48	160	76	50	0.66	175	394	128	0.33	461
	Strong	65	26	0.40	120	62	16	0.26	79	55	19	0.35	75	303	106	0.35	431
Narrative guidance	Fair	103	87	0.84	260	90	57	0.63	241	78	74	0.95	275	424	191	0.45	784
	Strong	67	30	0.45	125	53	19	0.36	80	46	19	0.41	49	303	106	0.35	304
Structured guidance	Fair	79	34	0.43	120	63	27	0.43	125	68	30	0.44	80	389	129	0.33	481
	Strong	86	41	0.48	170	53	17	0.32	60	81	63	0.78	225	324	121	0.37	345
Statistical	Fair	135	112	0.83	342	76	30	0.39	90	156	104	0.67	333	578	275	0.48	689
	Strong	116	97	0.83	341	77	36	0.47	126	93	76	0.82	275	485	225	0.46	724
Manager review																	
Senior decision	Fair	91	36	0.40	100	60	7	0.12	35	65	26	0.40	100	390	74	0.19	269
	Strong	59	23	0.39	90	48	17	0.35	49	70	70	1.00	306	342	144	0.42	500
Joint decision	Fair	87	37	0.43	100	82	52	0.63	191	96	51	0.53	191	353	128	0.36	544
	Strong	68	41	0.60	190	51	14	0.27	39	63	43	0.68	190	287	67	0.23	280

Figure 8.3
One-Way Analysis of Variance of Effect of Internal Control Treatment
on Sample Size Recommendations

Experiment	E-5 Packing Slip Comparison	E-6 Pricing Test	E-9 Posting Test	E-10 Confirmations
No guidance	Yes (α = .08)	Yes (α = .05)	No (α = .15)	Yes (α = .03)
Narrative guidance	No (α = .14)	Yes (α = .02)	No (α = .25)	Yes (α = .04)
Structured guidance	No* (α = .62)	No (α = .23)	No* (α = .56)	No (α = .18)
Statistical approach	No (α = .67)	No* (α = .90)	No (α = .14)	No (α = .36)
Manager review	No (α = .22)	Yes (α = .04)	Yes (α = .08)	Yes (α = .10)
Over all experiments	Yes (α = .05)	Yes (α = .005)	Yes (α = .025)	Yes (α = .005)

Note: Significant at $\alpha \leq .10$
* Average recommended sample sizes were larger for strong control treatment as compared to the fair control treatment.

Figure 8.4

Two-Way Analysis of Variance of Internal Control and Guidance/Approach

Differences Over All Valid Sample Size Decisions

Experimental Effects by Audit Procedure	F Value	Degrees of Freedom	Significance	Percent of Variance Explained (R^2)
E-5 Packing Slip Comparison				
Internal control	3.47	1, 130	α = .065	
Guidance/Approach	2.64	4, 130	α = .037	
Interaction	0.53	4, 130	Not Sig.	10.0%
E-6 Pricing Test				
Internal control	13.15	1, 136	α = .005	
Guidance/Approach	1.38	4, 136	Not Sig.	
Interaction	1.43	4, 136	Not Sig.	11.5%
E-9 Posting Test				
Internal control	5.95	1, 107	α = .016	
Guidance/Approach	4.07	4, 107	α = .004	
Interaction	1.20	4, 107	Not Sig.	16.6%
E-10 Confirmations				
Internal control	11.50	1, 135	α = .001	
Guidance/Approach	7.69	4, 135	α = .000	
Interaction	0.16	4, 135	Not Sig.	23.6%

Hypothesis H6 predicted a reduction in sample size variability given the additional guidance provided in the narrative-guidance, structured-guidance, statistical-approach, and manager-review experiments. The rationale for this hypothesis is based on an assumption that (1) some sort of ideal sample size exists and (2) given the relevant cues and objectives, seasoned professional judgment will approach the ideal. Guidance directs attention to the relevant cues and objectives. If observed judgments do concentrate around a single point, consensus is said to be high and variability low. High variability, then, indicates lack of consensus.

A problem with this type of analysis is the difficulty in obtaining an acceptable measure of variability (consensus). Figure 8.2, for example, contains three measures of variability—range, standard deviation, and coefficient of variation. Range indicates the difference between the highest and lowest recommended sample sizes. The largest ranges among the five experiments were 342 packing slip/invoice comparisons for E-5, 241 invoice price tests for E-6, 333 invoice posting tests for E9, and 784 confirmations for E-10. Such wide ranges may indicate significant risk of both unwarranted reliance and of overauditing, although drawing such an implication without a careful evaluation of the entire audit program is somewhat tenuous. Clearly, variability exists in terms of the subjects' range of recommended judgmental samples.

A second measure of variability presented in figure 8.2 is the standard deviation. If one divides the standard deviation of sample size recommendations by the mean sample size, a coefficient of variation (CV) results. Note that the CV is standardized by using the mean sample size, which facilitates comparison among different audit procedures. For example, in figure 8.2, the CV for the packing slip comparison in the no-guidance experiment is 60 percent, whereas it is only 33 percent for the confirmation procedure. As with the range measures, the CV measures in figure 8.2 indicate a significant amount of variability, with thirty-one of forty-eight coefficients exceeding 40 percent. A 40 percent CV indicates that roughly one-third of the sample size recommendations were at least 40 percent larger or 40 percent smaller than the average recommendation.[6]

In order to evaluate the effect of the experimental guidance and internal accounting control treatments on sample size variability, the CVs are ranked in figure 8.5, and an average ranking over the four audit procedures is calculated.

For hypothesis H6, which predicted reduced variability and greater consensus given greater guidance, to be supported, the rankings for the no-guidance experiment should be near 1. This would indicate the highest coefficient of variation. In fact, the no-guidance variability has the lowest average for the strong internal accounting control treatment and the second lowest for the fair treatment. Thus, hypothesis H6 is not supported.

The effect of the internal accounting control treatment on variability is also shown in figure 8.5. In phase 1 (no-guidance and narrative guidance) of these experiments, there was some limited evidence that consensus increased (that is, variability decreased) in the strong internal accounting control treatment. This effect was not sustained throughout the experiments, as the comparison of CVs for fair versus strong indicates in figure 8.5. In only eleven of twenty cases are the CVs for the strong treatment less than those for the fair treatment. Thus, neither the guidance nor the internal accounting control treatments consistently reduced variability in the subjects' sample size decisions.

EFFECT OF BEHAVIORAL FACTORS ON MEAN SAMPLE SIZE RECOMMENDATIONS

Halo Effect

A number of behavioral variables have been posited as being important in an auditor's information search and decision process. In chapter 6 the possibility of a halo effect was hypothesized (H3). A halo effect would be said to exist if an auditor reduced the sample size of substantive procedures because of improvements in the *general* internal accounting control environment even though no improvements in *specific*, relevant controls occurred. This was the case for audit procedure E-5, the packing slip comparison.

The halo effect hypothesis may be tested using the analysis of variance data contained in figure 8.3. If the halo effect is significant, the amount of variance explained for E-5 by classifying observations

Figure 8.5
Comparison of Variability of Sample Size Recommendations
Ranked in Terms of Coefficients of Variation (CV)

| | Audit Procedure | | | | | | | | | | | | | Average Ranks | |
| | E-5 Packing Slip Comparison | | | E-6 Pricing Test | | | E-9 Posting Test | | | E-10 Confirmations | | | | |
Guidance Treatment	Fair	Strong	S<F?	Fair	Strong	S<F?	Fair	Strong	S<F?	Fair	Strong	S<F?	Fair	Strong
No guidance	3	5	Yes	3	5	Yes	3	5	Yes	4.5	3.5	No	3.4	4.6
Narrative guidance	1	4	Yes	1.5	2	Yes	1	4	Yes	2	3.5	Yes	1.4	3.4
Structured guidance	4.5	3	No	4	3	Yes	5	2	No	4.5	2	No	4.5	2.5
Statistical approach	2	1	=	5	1	No	2	1	No	1	1	Yes	2.5	1
Manager review	4.5	2	No	1.5	4	Yes	4	3	No	3	4	Yes	3.3	3.3

Note: The rankings within the table are from the largest CV, 1 to the smallest CV, 5. The column labeled S<F? indicates whether the CV for the strong treatment is less than the CV for the fair treatment.

according to fair and strong would be significant. As shown in figure 8.2, most of the average sample sizes for E-5 (strong) are less than the average sample sizes for E-5 (fair). Yet, only in the no-guidance and overall-experiments cases are the differences statistically significant. Thus, if a halo effect exists, the guidance treatments seem to mitigate the effect. Additional evidence of this is provided in a later section of this chapter.

Anchoring Effect

The research situation also provided the opportunity to evaluate the effect of the anchoring heuristic hypothesized earlier (H4). Some suggestive, but not conclusive, evidence of anchoring was obtained by comparing the experimental subjects that worked under the strong treatment with a no-anchor control group (see figure 8.6).

The evidence is weak because the experimental situation for the no-anchor control group differed in terms of time allowed, an abridged version of the case was given, and there was no requirement for a written rationale memo. Given the experimental situation, it is impossible to determine what effect these variations had on the results. For three of the four procedures, subjects who had planned samples (anchors) recommended larger samples than did the control group, which had no planned samples, and the larger sample sizes lie between the planned sample sizes and the no-anchor recommendations. Also, in these three instances, the differences in sample sizes were statistically significant. The exception, E-6, the pricing test, where the two sample means are essentially the same, may be explained by the fact that the subjects' average recommendation equaled a firm-specific anchor for an attribute sample (see step E-6a in Appendix A). Some additional evidence of anchoring is contained in the subjects' rationale memos and in the protocol study discussed in chapter 11.

ANALYSIS OF SUBJECTS' EXPLICIT RATIONALE DERIVED FROM STRUCTURED DOCUMENTATION FORMS

As part of this study, research was conducted into the factors and decision processes that underlie auditors' sample size judgments. One approach

Figure 8.6
Recommended Sample Sizes With and Without Planned Sample (Anchor)
(Strong Control Treatment Only)

	E-5 Packing Slip Comparison		E-6 Pricing Test		E-9 Posting Test		E-10 Confirmations	
	Planned	No Planned	Planned	No Planned	Planned	No Planned	Planned	No Planned
This year's planned program	150	—	59	—	100	—	439	—
Field experiments:								
Mean sample	79	42	59	59	68	44	337	205
Significant difference?	Yes	—	No	—	Yes	—	Yes	—

was designed into the structured-guidance experiment in which subjects were required to explicate a number of factors that the normative analysis of the case deemed relevant. These factors were detailed in chapter 6 and included audit procedure objective, materiality, nature of audit procedure (substantive, compliance, or dual purpose), reliance placed on internal controls, and feasible range of samples. Thirty-five auditors completed the structured-guidance experiment. The results are summarized in figure 8.7.

The table includes the maximum sample size that subjects would consider if all factors pointed toward a large sample. Also included are the minimum sample sizes they would consider if all factors pointed toward a small sample and the procedure were to be included in the audit program. The difference between the maximum and minimum is a measure of the subjects' feasible range, which is defined to be their *cognitive width*.

Some of the variability (lack of consensus) discussed in the previous section can be explained in terms of differences between auditors in making some of these judgments. For example, the "reliance placed" judgment has a relatively high standard deviation of up to one on a four-point scale. Since sample size decisions are directly related to reliance judgments, variability in reliance logically leads to variability in sample size decisions.

Consider the results contained in figure 8.8, which shows the wide divergence in opinion about the nature of the packing slip comparison and the pricing tests. In both cases, subjects were almost evenly divided in regard to a substantive, compliance, or dual purpose interpretation of the test. The observed variability in the nature of test interpretation is another possible reason for lack of consensus among auditors.

Figure 8.8 also shows the sample size range, mean, and coefficient of variation according to the nature interpretation. The results of analysis of variance of the possible effect of nature interpretation on sample sizes is also given for the packing slip comparison, E-5, and the pricing test, E-6. In the case of E-5, the effect is not significant, but it is significant for E-6, in which, on the average, subjects recommended smaller sample sizes for the substantive interpretation.

Figure 8.7 also includes data concerning subjects' reliance judgments scored on a four-point scale. One would hypothesize that, except for the packing slip comparison, greater reliance would be indicated by subjects given the strong control treatment. In fact, as figure 8.9 shows, reliance was significantly greater. Also, negative (but statistically insignificant) correlations were observed between the sample size recommendations of these three procedures and the reliance decisions. The statistical insignificance of these correlations may indicate that a more complex decision process underlies sample size decisions than simply an inverse relation between reliance and sample size. Finally, figure 8.9 shows the lack of a halo effect for the packing slip comparison, since the reliance effect is not significant.

Internal control judgments could be sensitive to the range of feasible sample sizes that auditors consider. For instance, if an auditor specifies a narrow range of sample sizes, regardless of internal accounting controls, not much change in recommended sample sizes can be expected. In order to investigate such effects, a cognitive width analysis was performed. First, an investigation was conducted to check for significant internal accounting control effects on cognitive widths, even though the adequacy of internal accounting controls would not be expected to be related to subjectively determined maximum or minimum sample sizes as defined. Indeed, as figure 8.10 shows, no significant effect was observed.

Second, an analysis of variance was conducted on the sample sizes standardized by cognitive width. Standardization removes differences among subjects regarding ranges of samples they were considering. This facilitates evaluation of the effect that the internal control treatment had on moving the subjects' recommended sample size toward the high (1) or low (0) end of their cognitive width. For example, as is shown in figure 8.11, on the average, subjects with the fair treatment recommended confirmations at the midpoint (.51) of their cognitive widths.

With strong controls, their recommended sample sizes were at the lower (.38) end of their cognitive widths. As was the case with the nonstandardized sample sizes, the standardized sample sizes show no statistically significant internal accounting control effects.

Figure 8.7
Summary Statistics, Structured Documentation

Audit Procedure	Internal Control Treatment	Recommended Sample Size (SS)			Maximum SS Considered		Minimum SS Considered		Materiality 1=Material 3=Highly Material		Reliance Placed on Internal Controls 0=None 3=Very Great	
		μ	σ	R	μ	R	μ	R	μ	σ	μ	σ
E-5 Packing slip comparison	Fair	74.3	29.7	120	157	240	43	55	2.6	0.67	1.1	0.8
	Strong	84.9	42.9	170	163	250	48	85	2.7	0.68	1.4	0.8
E-6 Pricing test	Fair	62.1	27.9	125	91	275	43	50	2.8	0.60	1.5	0.6
	Strong	52.1	17.7	60	112	280	42	49	2.7	0.70	1.9	0.5
E-9 Posting test	Fair	65.2	29.5	80	125	225	45	55	2.8	0.40	1.0	0.7
	Strong	83.8	65.2	225	132	290	40	54	2.8	0.60	1.6	1.0
E-10 Confirmations	Fair	369	112	366	547	670	227	350	3.0	0.00	1.4	0.4
	Strong	318	122	345	637	2015	234	419	3.0	0.00	1.8	0.5

Notation: μ = mean, σ = standard deviation, R = range, SS = recommended sample size

Figure 8.8

Relationship Between Subjects' Interpretation of Nature of Audit Procedure
and Recommended Sample Sizes (Structured Documentation)

	Audit Procedure															
	E-5 Packing Slip Comparison				E-6 Pricing Test				E-9 Posting Test				E-10 Confirmations			
Nature of Interpretation	N	R	μ	CV	N	R	μ	CV	N	R	μ	CV	N	R	μ	CV
Substantive	7	65	84	0.25	8	49	45	0.44	16	230	79	0.72	21	355	346	0.32
Compliance	9	70	66	0.44	8	85	70	0.39	3	41	78	0.27	1	n/a	n/a	n/a
Dual purpose	12	150	86	0.53	10	60	56	0.32	2	34	42	0.57	4	331	293	0.58
ANOVA summary																
F Value	0.87				2.57				Not appropriate				Not appropriate			
Significance	Not significant				α = .097											

Notation: N = number of subjects, R = sample size range, μ = sample size mean, CV = coefficient of variation

Figure 8.9

Analysis of Effect of Internal Control Treatment on Reliance Judgment and
Correlation Between Reliance Judgment and Sample Size Recommendation
(Structured Guidance, Valid Subjects)

	Audit Procedure											
	E-5 Packing slip Comparison			E-6 Pricing Test			E-9 Posting Test			E-10 Confirmation		
	N	μ	CV	N	μ	CV	N	μ	CV	N	μ	CV
Treatment												
Fair controls	17	1.20	0.70	17	1.50	0.41	17	1.10	0.66	18	1.40	0.28
Strong controls	16	1.40	0.56	16	1.90	0.27	14	1.60	0.61	16	1.80	0.31
T-Test	0.71			1.88			1.63			2.31		
Significance of treatment	Not significant			$\alpha = .10$			$\alpha = .10$			$\alpha = .10$		
Correlation of reliance and sample size	.228			-.227			-.295			-.140		
Significance of correlation	Not significant			Not significant			Not significant			Not significant		

Note: Question F in the structured documentation memo stated, "In recommending a sample size, how much reliance are you placing on internal controls?"

```
        None      Some      Substantial    Very great
```

The replies were scaled from 0 for "None" to 3 for "Very great."
Notation: See figure 8.8

Figure 8.10

Analysis of Effect of Internal Control Treatment on Cognitive Widths
Specified by Subjects for Structured-Guidance Experiment

	Treatment								Significance of Treatment	
	Fair Controls				Strong Controls				ANOVA F Value	Significant? ($\alpha \leq .10$)
	N	R	μ	CV	N	R	μ	CV		
E-5: Packing slip comparison	13	255	120	0.70	13	268	104	0.82	1.20	No
E-6: Pricing test	7	265	78	1.18	8	270	98	0.98	0.03	No
E-9: Posting test	8	239	99	0.86	12	270	97	0.88	0.55	No
E-10: Confirmations	9	606	346	0.60	10	2195	423	1.58	0.32	No

Notation: See figure 8.8

VARIABILITY IN SUBJECTS' SPECIFICATION
OF STATISTICAL SAMPLING PARAMETERS

Another possible rationale for the observed variability in subjects' sample sizes lies in their judgments concerning the parameters that underlie statistical samples. Variability in the specification of such parameters is apparent in figure 8.12, which is based on the statistical approach data. For the statistical approach, subjects determined judgmentally several dollar unit sample parameters for procedure E-10, confirmation of accounts receivable. Their judgments concerning the parameters—beta risk, alpha risk, materiality, and acceptable amount of overstatement—had coefficients of variation ranging between 28 and 86 percent. The range of chosen values for materiality was from $10,500 to $61,000 and for beta risk from 5 percent to 50 percent. Evidence of such differences in auditors' judgments may help explain the variability both in the statistical approach and in the entire set of experiments.

Figure 8.12 also shows the analysis of variance results for the effect that differences in the internal accounting controls had on the parameter judgments. As would be expected, in the case of beta risk this effect is significant. Those subjects given the strong compliance test results established a beta risk nine percent higher on the average than those subjects with the fair compliance test results.

ANALYSIS OF SUBJECT DEMOGRAPHICS

As a final attempt to explain the observed differences in sample size recommendations, demographic data were collected and analyzed, primarily for phase 1, no-guidance and narrative-guidance, subjects. Figure 8.13 contains a summary of subject demographics. More detail was collected for phase I subjects. Because no significant demographic effects were observed, only specialized training and experience data were obtained for subsequent experiments.

Figure 8.13 shows that, on the average, the seniors had over three years of audit experience, with about two years of commercial experience (in contrast to experience with financial institutions, government, and so forth). Except for the statistical approach, the majority of subjects had no

Figure 8.11
Analysis of the Effect of the Internal Control Treatment
on Subjects' Planned Sample Sizes Standardized by Cognitive
Width for Structured-Guidance Experiment

| | Treatment | | | | | | | | Significance of Treatment | |
| | Fair Controls | | | | Strong Controls | | | | | Difference in Means Significant? (α≤.10) |
	N	R	μ	CV	N	R	μ	CV	T Value	
E-5: Packing slip comparison	13	1	0.27	1.70	13	1.0	0.40	0.73	1.09	No
E-6: Pricing test	7	1	0.32	1.13	8	0.9	0.29	1.07	0.18	No
E-9: Posting test	8	1	0.24	1.41	12	1.0	0.37	1.02	0.75	No
E-10: Confirmations	9	1	0.51	0.63	10	1.9	0.38	1.70	0.56	No

Notation: See figure 8.8

Figure 8.12
Analysis of the Effect of Internal Control Treatment on
Subjects' Specification of Dollar Unit Sample Parameters
for Audit Procedure E-10

| | Treatment | | | | | | | | Significance of Treatment Difference in Means | |
| | Fair Controls | | | | Strong Controls | | | | | Significant? ($\alpha \leq .10$) |
	N	R	μ	CV	N	R	μ	CV	T Value	
E-5: Packing slip comparison	16	0.34	0.14	0.85	15	0.45	0.23	0.72	1.70	Yes
E-6: Pricing test	15	0.05	0.07	0.36	13	0.15	0.07	0.60	0.23	No
E-9: Posting test	16	$50,500	$20,140	0.55	15	$24,000	$18,625	0.30	0.59	No
E-10: Confirmations	15	$ 8,480	$ 4,143	0.52	13	$ 4,800	$ 3,809	0.28	0.50	No

specialized statistical or computer training. The more detailed data collected on the no-guidance and narrative-guidance subjects indicate a rather homogeneous population in terms of audit experience, audit-level courses taken, and client mix.

To evaluate possible demographic effects, such as differences in specialized training, one-way analysis of variance was applied to the sample size decisions for phase 1 subjects. Figure 8.14 shows that in only one case is a significant amount of variance explained.[7] Analysis of covariance indicated some significant commercial and audit experience effects on sample size decisions for the statistical approach and the manager-review experiments. However, the preponderance of evidence indicates that the demographic variables tested were not significant determinants of differences in, or variability of, sample size recommendations.

ANALYSIS LIMITATIONS

The analysis used in this chapter is based on parametric statistics and on the assumptions that underlie analysis of variance and the other tests that were utilized. The assumption most frequently violated in the observed data was that of equal variance, which is that the standard deviations of the data sets are approximately equal (see figure 8-2). This particular violation does not result in significant risk of erroneous conclusions if the sample sizes are relatively equal. The experimental design summarized in figure 7.1 shows that the cell sizes were essentially equal.

A second limitation of any inferences based on this chapter concerns the test of anchoring. As was noted earlier, the no-anchor control group differed from the experimental group in several ways in addition to not being supplied with planned sample sizes. Thus, while the data support the anchoring hypothesis, it is not conclusive. Other possible limitations in research design are noted in earlier chapters.

Figure 8.13
Summary of Demographic Information

	No guidance Narrative Guidance Combined	Structured Guidance	Statistical Approach	Manager Review	
				Seniors	Managers
Experience in years					
Up to 2.5	10				
2.5 - 3.0	27				
3.5 - 4.0	20				
4.5 or more	16				
	73				
Average experience (years)	3.3	2.0	4.1	3.2	6.6
Specialized training					
Computer audit specialist (CAS)	16	1	6	4	9
Statistical audit specialist (SAS)	6	0	34	2	5
No specialized training	51	35	0	24	17
Highest Audit Course Taken					
Staff level	1				
Senior level	3				
Supervising senior level	64				
Data not available	5				
	73				

Figure 8.13 (continued)
Summary of Demographic Information

	No guidance Narrative Guidance Combined	Structured Guidance	Statistical Approach	Manager Review	
				Seniors	Managers
Commercial Experience					
None	3				
Some	8				
Moderate	28				
Extensive	30				
Data not available	4				
	73				
Average commercial experience (years)	2.3	1.8	2.1	1.9	1.8
Client Mix Experience					
Primarily small clients	5				
Mixed	53				
Primarily large clients	11				
Data not available	4				
	73				

Figure 8.14
Analysis of Variance of Sample Size Decisions
by Demographic Factors for No-Guidance and
Narrative-Guidance Experiments

Possible Explanatory Variable	E-5 Packing Slip Comparison	E-6 Pricing Test	E-9 Posting Test	E-10 Confirmations
Experience Factors				
1. Years of experience	$F = 1.09$ (No)	$F = 1.08$ (No)	$F = 0.33$ (No)	$F = 1.54$ (No)
2. Commercial experience (some, moderate, extensive)	$F = 0.06$ (No)	$F = 0.23$ (No)	$F = 0.88$ (No)	$F = 1.48$ (No)
3. Client mix experience (small, mixed, large clients)	$F = 0.56$ (No)	$F = 0.95$ (No)	$F = 0.17$ (No)	$F = 0.57$ (No)
Training Factors				
1. Specialized statistical or computer schools	$F = 0.43$ (No)	$F = 0.92$ (No)	$F = 0.17$ (No)	$F = 0.86$ (No)
2. Local office internal control evaluation training session	$F = 0.11$ (No)	$F = 0.02$ (No)	$F = 0.15$ (No)	$F = 1.33$ (No)
3. Local office statistical program	$F = 0.39$ (No)	$F = 1.90$ (No)	$F = 1.93$ (No)	$F = 0.65$ (No)
Miscellaneous				
1. Local office effects	$F = 0.81$ (No)	$F = 1.37$ (No)	$F = 2.54$ (Yes)	$F = 0.75$ (No)

Note: F values and significance at $\alpha \leq .10$

SUMMARY

This chapter has presented statistical results of the effect of various factors on auditors' sample size recommendations. These decisions were found to be significantly affected by differences in internal accounting control treatments and were found to exhibit a great deal of variability among auditors. Tests of possible auditor behavioral heuristics led to evidence of an anchoring heuristic, but a halo effect observed in the early experiments seemed to be mitigated by guidance. In addition, differences in the guidance provided were significant determinants of differences in sample size decisions. The analyses also included an attempt to explain sample size variability in terms of a number of experimental and behavioral factors. In general, few of these variables were found to be related to sample size variability. A summary of the hypothesis test results is as follows:

Hypothesis   Results

Experimental differences in Average Sample Sizes

Hypothesis	Results
H1: General effect of improving internal accounting controls	Generally supported but no statistical procedures performed
H2: Differential effect of strong control treatment	Significant over all experiments. Mixed results for individual treatments.
H5: General guidance effect on mean sample sizes	Guidance effects significant for three of four procedures

Experimental Differences in the Variability of Sample Size Recommendations

H6: Guidance effect on variability of sample size recommendations	Not supported

Behavioral tendencies

H3: Halo effect	Significant for no-guidance and over-all-experiments cases only
H4: Anchoring effect	Significant for three of four procedures

Other hypotheses

H8: Interaction effect	No significant interaction effects on variability of samples

DISCUSSION OF RESULTS

Experimental Differences in Average Sample Sizes

H1: General Effect of Improving Internal Accounting Controls. For both the fair and strong treatments, the improvements of specific controls relevant to the price test, the posting test, and the confirmation procedure are expected to result in reduced sample size recommendations.

Generally supported but no statistical procedures were performed because a control group was not tested. Only the strong treatment indicates consistent reduction over all procedures.

H2: Differential Effect of Strong Control Treatment. For the price test, the posting test, and the confirmation procedure, recommended sample sizes of subjects receiving the strong internal control compliance test results are expected to be significantly smaller than those of subjects receiving the fair treatment.

One-way ANOVA results indicate that, over all experiments, sample sizes are significantly smaller for the strong treatment than for the fair treatment. One-way ANOVA results for the guidance treatment indicate significant differences for only seven of fifteen cases. Two-way ANOVA results indicate internal accounting control effects to be significant and in the expected directions.

H5: General Guidance Effect on Mean Sample Sizes. The various guidance treatments are not expected to have any significant effects on recommended sample sizes.

Two-way ANOVA results indicate that guidance effects are significant for three of four procedures. Guidance differences may result from larger sample size recommendations for the statistical approach experiment.

Experimental Differences in the Variability of Sample Size Recommendations

H6: Guidance Effect on Variability of Sample Size Recommendations. Narrative guidance, structured guidance, the statistical approach, and manager review are all expected to result in reduced variability in sample size recommendations.

Based on a ranking by control treatment of the average coefficients of variation for the four procedures, hypothesized reductions in variability are not supported.

Behavioral Tendencies

H3: Halo Effect. For the packing slip comparison, the improvement in the general control environment is expected to result in significantly smaller sample size recommendations for subjects receiving the strong control treatment than those of subjects receiving the fair treatment.

One-way ANOVA results indicate significant differences for the no-guidance and the over-all-experiments cases only. Guidance treatments may serve to mitigate the halo effect.

H4: Anchoring Effect. In contrast with a control group receiving no planned sample sizes, subjects are expected to begin adjusting from the originally planned sample sizes. This should result in significant differences in sample size recommendations between the subjects and the control group.

Results of t-tests indicate significant differences for three of four procedures with the group provided an anchor recommending larger sample sizes than those recommended by the control group. The nature of the fourth test — an attribute test — may have influenced the lack of significantly different sample size recommendations for that test.

Other Hypotheses

H8: Interaction Effects. The internal accounting control and guidance treatments are not expected to have any explicit interaction effects on either sample sizes or rationale memos.

Two-way ANOVA results indicate no significant interaction effects on the variability of samples.

NOTES

1. The subject's rationale memos indicated that procedures were eliminated primarily because the auditor received "little comfort" (i.e. no significant information content) from the procedure or because other procedures could be substituted.

2. A positive confirmation requests a reply whether the account is in error or not, whereas a negative confirmation requests a reply only if the account is incorrect.

3. See chapter 7 for explicit statement of hypothesis H1 and others.

4. In other words, no control group used the weak compliance test results reported in the Olde Oak case for the previous audit period.

5. Recall that no significant difference is expected for the packing slip comparison if no relevant control improved.

6. If a population is normally distributed, almost two-thirds of the observations lie within one standard deviation. Thus, about one-third lie outside of plus-or-minus one standard deviation.

7. "Local office effects" classified subjects according to the office (city) to which they reported.

CHAPTER 9

Experimental Results: A *Synthetic a Posteriori* Modeling Approach of the Auditors' Sample Size Decisions[1]

The results of the previous chapter indicated, among other things, that there was a significant amount of unexplained variability in auditors' decisions. Significant variability measured in terms of both ranges and coefficients of variation were observed in the five related experiments. More importantly perhaps, much of the observed variability was not attributable to either the experimental variables or the interpersonal differences. Analysis of variance showed that the two experimentally controlled variables (compliance test results and auditor guidance) accounted for only 10.0 to 23.6 percent of the observed variance in the auditors' four scope decisions. These and other results imply that additional multivariate analysis may be useful regarding the way in which auditors weight various informational, organizational, and behavioral cues and combine them in order to reach a judgment.

Another important issue raised in earlier chapters is the adequacy of auditor judgment documentation. The adequacy issue is addressed in this chapter by attempting to use two forms of auditor rationale documentation to build improved models of auditor judgments. As will be seen, models that explain more variance and exhibit predictive validity can be derived.

ALTERNATIVE APPROACHES TO THE
MODELING OF JUDGMENT AND DECISIONS

Interest in the modeling of decisions has been evident in audit research for many years. Audit judgment research has examined auditor decision making from several perspectives, with experimentation being the primary methodology used. This type of research may be classified as *synthetic a posteriori.*[2]

SYNTHETIC A POSTERIORI MODELS

Models derived through observation (i.e. *a posteriori*) are of interest in auditing because complexity makes the derivation of analytical models difficult. Within this class, the models may be *idiographic* (individual specific) or *nomothetic* (based on common features shared by individuals). Little idiographic judgment modeling research has been published in accounting and auditing.[3]

The main purpose of this chapter is to present the results of a *synthetic a posteriori* modeling approach to auditor judgments. In general, this approach involves deriving models using multivariate statistical techniques applied to repeated measures of auditor judgments (as dependent variables) and various input cues, demographics or other possible independent (explanatory) variables. Two sets of data with which to build these models are discussed below and summarized in figure 9.1.

Figure 9.1
Variables Used to Analyze Concurrent Documentation

Variable 1	=	Nature of test - substantive
Variable 2	=	Nature of test - compliance
Variable 3	=	Materiality - Was the account balance the audit procedure relates to material or immaterial?
Variable 4	=	Reliance placed - In recommending sample sizes for this audit procedure, are you placing some or no reliance on the system of internal accounting controls?

Variable 5	=	Maximum sample size - The largest sample size you would recommend if all factors pointed towards a large sample.
Variable 6	=	Minimum sample size - The smallest sample size you would recommend if all factors pointed towards a small sample size and you still decide to perform the procedure.
Variable 7	=	Experimental treatment - Fair or strong as defined in chapter 5.

DATA SUMMARY

Recall that the dependent variable data sets consist of sample size judgments of audit seniors and supervisors. As subjects completed the task, two types of documentation were prepared. These can be viewed as independent variables which may be correlated with sample size decisions. *Retrospective documentation* (see chapter 5 for details) consisted of open-ended rationale memos prepared after the auditors had arrived at their sample size recommendations. *Concurrent documentation* consisted of filling out detailed questionnaires as each subject was gathering data and reaching a sample size decision.

Timing was the essential difference between the two documentation tasks. That is, in the concurrent documentation task, auditors were asked to consider various factors and to indicate judgments concerning these factors in reaching their explicit sample size judgments. On the other hand, the retrospective documentation task required the auditors to recall, after the fact, which factors had influenced their sample size recommendations.

RESEARCH QUESTIONS

Based on the data from the above experimental setting, and the desire to consider the issues of modeling auditor judgment and appraising documentation adequacy, the following additional research questions were developed:

1. What is the nature of the decision (judgment) models underlying sample size judgments based on concurrent and retrospective documentation techniques?
2. What is the relative importance of the various factors in the models?
3. Are the derived cue weights assigned to the various factors stable across audit procedures?
4. Do the descriptive, derived models have predictive validity?
5. What are the effects of individual auditor differences on the model parameters?
6. Are there significant differences between the concurrent documentation and the retrospective documentation models? If so, what is the basis of similarities/dissimilarities in the two models?

The above research questions are concerned with aggregate or group models of auditor judgments, and thus are *nomothetic* in methodological terms.

DATA ANALYSIS METHODS AND RESULTS

The research questions of the previous section reflect several important issues underlying the modeling approach. These issues, broadly stated, are categorized as follows :

1. Model search and development—research questions 1, 2, 3.
2. Model interpretability—research questions 2, 3.
3. Model predictive ability—research question 4.
4. Model representativeness: nomothetic versus idiographic considerations—research question 5.
5. Documentation timing effects—research question 6.

Each of these issues is now discussed with a description of the analyses utilized in their assessment and the ensuing results. A discussion of the results constitutes the final section of this chapter.

MODEL SEARCH AND DEVELOPMENT

The starting point for model development is an assessment of the nature of the underlying data. As previously stated, the two documentation approaches required the auditors to indicate their use of, reliance on, and/or judgments concerning certain factors in reaching a sample size decision.

Factors included in the content analysis dictionary (see figure 10.2) for the retrospective documentation task are:

1. Audit test objectives
2. General and specific control references
3. Cost
4. Risk
5. Other audit evidence
6. Nature and timing of the test
7. Nature of the test: compliance, substantive, or dual purpose.

For the concurrent documentation task, the questionnaire elicited judgments are:

1. Nature of the audit test: compliance, substantive, or dual purpose
2. Materiality
3. Degree of reliance
4. Sample size range indicated by maximum sample size and minimum sample size.

The majority of the data are binary coded with a "1" indicating reference to or reliance on a factor in the documentation task and a "0" indicating no reference. For the concurrent documentation task, minimum and maximum sample sizes were ratio scaled.

In addition to the referenced factors, demographic information was gathered and evaluated for the retrospective documentation task. This information is included in this study to determine if additional variance can be explained. The demographic factors are:

1. Actual number of years of audit experience (ratio scaled by actual years)
2. Specialist status (coded 0 if not a specialist, 1 if computer or statistical audit specialist)
3. Special firm computer audit training course (coded 0 if no, 1 if yes)
4. Local office internal control training course (coded 0 if no, 1 if yes)
5. Local office statistical training course (coded 0 if no, 1 if yes)
6. Commercial experience (coded 0 if none, 3 if extensive)
7. Number of audit level training courses (coded in intervals: 0 if lowest and 4 if highest)
8. Client mix (coded 1 if primarily small, 3 if primarily large).

One additional information factor was included and assessed in the model development—binary coded data reflecting the experimental treatments (0 if internal controls were "fair", 1 if "strong"). This factor was included since between 10 and 24 percent of the sample size judgment variance has been previously explained by this experimental treatment (see chapter 8).

Given the nature of the mostly categorical data, the general linear statistical modeling approach was deemed to be appropriate for assessing research questions 1, 2 and 3. Two special cases of the models were evaluated for relevance, ANOVA and regression, with the regression modeling approach being selected. The regression approach is a more general approach than ANOVA and can accommodate many independent variables, unequal sample sizes (for combination of reference and demographic factors), and can be analyzed by computer programs primarily designed to evaluate the "importance of the variables" question implied by research question 2.

The basic model development approach consisted of three steps:

1. Fit the full model to the data assuming only main effects, that is, no interactions between the factors.
2. Based on the model in step 1, select those combinations of factors that provide the "best" reduced model, assuming only main

effects, where "best" is defined as the model with the lowest Mallows' Cp.[4]

3. Fit the reduced model assuming interactions. Using Mallows' Cp, select those combinations of factors that provide the best reduced model.

These three steps were performed for each of the four audit procedures (E-5, E-6, E-9, E-10) over each of the two documentation approaches (retrospective, concurrent).

The hypothesized full model underlying the retrospective documentation task is:

$$Y = \sum_{k=0}^{18} \beta_k X_{ik} + \epsilon_i \qquad (9.1)$$

where $X_{i0} \equiv 1$, $I = 1, \ldots, n$, and where:

$$
\begin{aligned}
Y &= \text{observed sample size judgment} \\
\beta_0 &= \text{combination of factors at their lowest level} \\
\beta_1 \ldots \beta_{18} &= \text{cue weighting coefficients to be estimated for} \\
& \quad \text{each factor} \\
X_{i1} \ldots X_{i9} &= \text{internal accounting control reference factors in} \\
& \quad \text{the experimental task} \\
X_{i9} \ldots X_{i18} &= \text{demographic factors} \\
X_{i18} &= \text{treatment effect factor}
\end{aligned}
$$

The correspondence of the model terms and reference and control factors is shown in figure 9.2.

Figure 9.2
Relationship of Model Elements to Retrospective and
Concurrent Documentation Factors

A. Retrospective Documentation — Full Model

$$Y = \sum_{k=1}^{18} \beta_k X_{ik} + \epsilon_i$$

X_1 = Audit Test Objectives Specified

X_2 = General and Specific Control References

X_3 = Cost Considerations

X_4 = Risk Considerations

X_5 = Other Audit Evidence

X_6 = Nature and Timing of the Test

X_7 = Nature of the Test – Substantive

X_8 = Nature of the Test – Compliance

X_9 = Compliance Test Results

X_{10} = Years of Audit Experience

X_{11} = Specialist Status

X_{12} = Audit Level Training Courses Completed

X_{14} = Local Office Internal Control Training

X_{13} = Firm Computer Audit Training

X_{15} = Local Office Statistical Training

X_{16} = Commercial Experience

X_{17} = Client Mix

X_{18} = Experimental Treatment

B. Concurrent Documentation — Full Model

$$Y = \sum_{k=1}^{7} \beta_k X_{ik} + \epsilon_i$$

X_1 = Nature of the Test – Substantive

X_2 = Nature of the Test – Compliance

X_3 = Materiality of Account Being Audited

X_4 = Reliance Placed on System of Internal Accounting Controls

X_5 = Maximum Sample Size

X_6 = Minimum Sample Size

X_7 = Experimental Treatment

The full hypothesized model underlying the concurrent documentation task (see figure 9.2) is:

$$Y = \sum_{k=0}^{7} \beta_k X_{ik} + \epsilon_i \qquad (9.2)$$

where $X_{io} \equiv 1$, $I = 1, \ldots, n$ and where:

$$
\begin{array}{rcl}
Y & = & \text{observed sample size judgment} \\
\beta_0 & = & \text{combination of factors at their lowest level} \\
\beta_1 \ldots \beta_7 & = & \text{cue weighting coefficients to be estimated for each} \\
& & \text{factor} \\
X_{i1} \ldots X_{i7} & = & \text{factors referenced in the experimental task}
\end{array}
$$

The hypothesized reduced models for both the concurrent and retrospective tasks will be of the general form:

$$Y = \sum_{k=0}^{P-1} \beta_k X_{ik} + \sum_{k=1}^{n} \beta_k K_{ik} X_{k+1} + \epsilon_i \qquad (9.3)$$

$$
\begin{array}{rrcl}
\text{where:} & Y & = & \text{observed sample size judgment} \\
& \beta_0 & = & \text{combination of factors at their lowest level} \\
& \beta_1 \ldots \beta_n & = & \text{cue weighting coefficients to be estimated for each} \\
& & & \text{factor} \\
& X_{i1} \ldots X_{in} & = & \text{control reference, demographic, and treatment} \\
& & & \text{factors} \\
& X_{ik} \ldots X_{ik+1} & = & \text{interaction factors}
\end{array}
$$

In conjunction with fitting the full and reduced model steps, all of the control reference factors, some demographic factors (retrospective task only), and the treatment factor are qualitative. This means that there is no statistical relation between these factors and the dependent variable (Y) in the regression models. Therefore, nothing can be stated regarding the type of statistical response function such as linear or polynomial. If only these qualitative factors are present in the reduced models, these regression models are analogous to ANOVA models. On the other hand, if some or all of the quantitative (interval scaled) demographic factors are represented in the model with the qualitative factors, these models become analogous to analysis of covariance (ANCOVA) models provided certain assumptions are met. In the ANCOVA models, there is a hypothesized statistical relation between the qualitatively scaled factors (covariates) and the dependent variable. A critical assumption of the ANCOVA models is that of no interaction between the quantitatively scaled and qualitatively scaled factors. If these interactions are present, then separate regression models must be developed for each level of the quantitatively scaled factor. Thus, with reference to research question 1, there are a variety of potential models which may help understand auditor sample size judgments.

To further evaluate research question 1, steps 2 and 3 of the model building process must be undertaken. The goal of fitting reduced models to the data is to find the best combination of control reference, demographic, and treatment factors that, in a statistical and judgmental sense, parsimoniously represent the data. Steps 2 and 3 were undertaken for each of the four audit procedures over each of the two tasks.

Research question 2, regarding the relative importance of the final set of model factors, is answered by evaluating the reduced models developed for research question 1. Criteria for examining the relative importance of the factors include the marginal contribution of each factor to overall R^2 (percentage of variance explained), t-statistics for significance on each factor coefficient, and tolerance levels of each factor.[5]

Research question 3 is concerned with the stability of the regression model factors and parameters over each of the four audit procedures (E-5, E-6, E-9, E-10) given a particular documentation approach (e.g. retrospective). Criteria utilized for evaluation of the results include a comparison of the commonality of the control reference and demographic factors across procedures, an examination of the relative magnitude of the regression model parameters, and an examination of the mathematical sign on the parameters across the four audit procedures. If audit judgment models are the same across audit procedures, the same reference factors should be represent in all procedures and the coefficients of the factors in the regression model should be of the same order of magnitude and display the same sign.

RESULTS: MODEL SEARCH AND DEVELOPMENT

Figure 9.3 presents the summary of the results of reducing the full model considering only main effects (steps 1 and 2 of the previous section). As noted, the variance explained in the models (adjusted R^2) is relatively low, but much higher than that found in chapters 7 and 8, even though in all cases the overall regression models are highly significant.

Figure 9.4 shows the results of the analysis of the reduced models of figure 9.3, when interaction terms are built into the models. All procedures except E-9 retrospective and E-10 concurrent show significant increases (13% to 220%) in variance explained, and show a maintained or improved level of overall significance of the regression models.

Also, as may be noted in figure 9.3 and figure 9.4 and summarized in figure 9.5, the model elements do vary across audit procedures with few common model elements found across procedures. For example, for the retrospective documentation approach (see figure 9.5), *Nature and timing* in both procedures E-5 and E-10 and its parameters are of the same order of magnitude and display the same sign. *Other audit evidence* (retrospective) appears in procedures E-5 and E-9 and its parameters are of the same order of magnitude and displays the same sign across procedures. On the other hand, *Experimental treatment* (retrospective) appears in procedures E-5, E-6 and E-10 and its parameters are of the same order of magnitude and display the same sign for procedures E-5 and E-10 but differ substantially for procedure E-6. In the instances where the same model elements are found over the procedures, the signs and relative magnitude of the model parameters appear to be fairly stable, although not always, as discussed above.

All of the resulting models over three procedures (E-5, E-6, E-9) for the retrospective documentation task appear to be regression analogues of the ANOVA model; that is, all factors in the model are qualitative. For procedure E-10, two interval scaled factors appear in the model, and thus, this model appears to be the regression analogue to the ANCOVA model. Tests of the assumptions of the ANCOVA model, particularly those of parallel response surfaces, were negative indicating that significant interactions between qualitatively and quantitatively scaled factors were present. Thus, separate regression response functions exist with different slopes and intercepts for each level of the quantitatively scaled factors.

Figure 9.3
Summary Results of Main Effects, Full Model Reduction Based on Mallow's Cp Criterion for Four Audit Procedures Across Two Tasks

Retrospective Documentation Task

Original Factors in the Model

Reduced Model Factors for Four Audit Procedures

Control Reference	E-5 (Comparison)		E-6 (Pricing)		E-9 (Posting)		E-10 (Confirmation)	
	Regression Parameter	Standardized Parameter	Regression Parameter	Standardized Parameter	Regression Parameter	Standardized Parameter	Regression Parameter	Standardized Parameter
Audit Test Objectives				30.69	0.33		118.26	0.27
General and Specific Control References	34.83	0.28						
Cost								
Risk								
Other Audit Evidence	-20.15	-0.17	-19.23	-0.20	-31.51	-0.30		
Nature and Timing of the Test	33.69	0.22	18.02	0.18				
Nature of Test – Substantive			55.72	0.59	34.73	0.17	188.92	0.38
Nature of Test – Compliance			44.54	0.49				
Compliance Test Results								

Figure 9.3 (continued)

Retrospective Documentation Task

Original Factors in the Model

Reduced Model Factors for Four Audit Procedures

Demographics	E-5 (Comparison) Regression Parameter	E-5 (Comparison) Standardized Parameter	E-6 (Pricing) Regression Parameter	E-6 (Pricing) Standardized Parameter	E-9 (Posting) Regression Parameter	E-9 (Posting) Standardized Parameter	E-10 (Confirmation) Regression Parameter	E-10 (Confirmation) Standardized Parameter
Years of Audit Experience							-58.47	-0.40
Specialist Status			10.31	0.20			39.28	0.27
Audit Level Training								
Firm Internal Control Training								
Local Office Internal Control Training								
Commercial Experience								
Client Mix			-11.74	-0.18				
Treatment Effect								
Experimental Treatment	-31.80	-0.27	-31.56	-0.36			-72.38	-0.23
R^2	0.15		0.40		0.13		0.43	
Adjusted R^2	0.10		0.32		0.10		0.38	
F-Statistic	3.01		5.30		5.10		8.96	
Significance	0.02		0.00		0.01		0.00	

Figure 9.3 (continued)

Concurrent Documentation Task

Original Factors
in the Model

Reduced Model Factors for Four Audit Procedures

Control Questionnaire Factors	E-5 (Comparison)		E-6 (Pricing)		E-9 (Posting)		E-10 (Confirmation)	
	Regression Parameter	Standardized Parameter	Regression Parameter	Standardized Parameter	Regression Parameter	Standardized Parameter	Regression Parameter	Standardized Parameter
Nature of test - substantive	-20.47	-0.24	19.58	0.32				
Nature of test - compliance								
Materiality of account							323.13	0.13
Reliance placed on controls								
Maximum sample size judgment		0.19	0.52	0.35	0.55			
Minimum sample size judgment 0.52			0.38			0.51	0.44	
Nature of the test compliance	0.32	0.49						

Figure 9.3 (continued)

Concurrent Documentation Task (continued)

Reduced Model Factors for Four Audit Procedures

Original Factors
in the Model

	E-5 (Comparison)		E-6 (Pricing)		E-9 (Posting)		E-10 (Confirmation)	
Control Questionnaire Factors (Continued)	Regression Parameter	Standardized Parameter	Regression Parameter	Standardized Parameter	Regression Parameter	Standardized Parameter	Regression Parameter	Standardized Parameter
Treatment Effect								
Experimental Treatment	12.28		0.33		-15.25		-0.27	
R^2	0.35		0.59		0.30		0.28	
Adjusted R^2	0.28		0.53		0.27		0.23	
F-Statistic	5.05		9.89		12.75		5.64	
Significance	0.01		0.00		0.00		0.01	

Figure 9.4
Summary of Reduced Model Parameters with Interaction Terms over Four Audit Procedures Across Two Tasks

Procedure E-5 (Comparisons) Retrospective Documentation

Model Elements	Model Parameters	Standardized Model Parameters	2-Tail Significance	Contribution to R^2	Tolerance
Other Audit Evidence	-16.61	-0.27	0.01	0.06	0.82
Treatment Effect	-12.82	-0.27	0.06	0.04	0.78
Nature and Timing	21.31	0.28	0.03	0.05	0.62
Control Reference/Nature and Timing	47.22	0.33	0.02	0.06	0.50
Control Reference/Other Audit Evidence	28.64	0.31	0.01	0.07	0.72
Control Reference/Other Audit Evidence/ Nature and Timing	-64.97	-0.28	0.06	0.04	0.47
Control Reference/Treatment Effect/ Nature and Timing	-51.37	-0.38	0.00	0.08	0.51
Other Audit Evidence/Treatment Effect/ Nature and Timing	77.65	0.34	0.01	0.07	0.59
Combination of Factors at their Lowest Level	78.59	1.306	0.00	—	—

Overall Model E-5 Summary Statistics

Mean value of dependent variable - sample size judgment:	67.52		
Coefficient of Variation of dependent variable:	0.89		
Overall R^2	0.39	F-Statistic	4.53
Adjusted R^2	0.31	Significance	0.00
Improvement in Adjusted R^2 over main effects model:	220%		

Figure 9-4 (continued)

Procedure E-6 (Pricing Test)

Model Elements	Model Parameters	Standardized Model Parameters	2-Tail Significance	Contribution to R²	Tolerance
Experimental treatment	83.85	0.96	0.01	0.05	0.06
Nature of test–substantive	85.62	0.90	0.00	0.09	0.11
Nature of test–compliance	80.96	0.89	0.00	0.12	0.15
Audit test objectives/Nature of test –substantive	40.88	0.24	0.02	0.04	0.76
Audit test objectives/Audit level training 32.04	0.37	0.00	0.09	0.67	
Other audit evidence/Nature of test –substantive	-42.18	-0.24	0.01	0.05	0.78
Nature of test–substantive/Nature and timing	27.89	0.20	0.06	0.03	0.64
Nature of test–substantive/Experimental treatment	-97.37	-0.92	0.00	0.06	0.07
Nature of test–compliance/Audit level training	-11.51	-0.19	0.09	0.02	0.62
Nature of test–compliance/Experimental treatment	-85.74	-0.84	0.01	0.06	0.08
Compliance test results/Experimental treatment	-16.56	-0.42	0.02	0.04	0.22

Overall Model E-6 Summary Statistics

Mean value of dependent variable - sample size judgment	63.60		
Coefficient of variation of dependent variable:	0.69		
Overall R²	0.57	F-Statistic	7.33
Adjusted R²	0.49	Significance	0.00
Improvement in Adjusted R² over main effects model:	53%		

Figure 9-4 (continued)

Procedure E-9 (Posting Test)

Model Elements	Model Parameters	Standardized Model Parameters	2-Tail Significance	Contribution to R^2	Tolerance
Other audit evidence	-31.51	-0.30	0.01	0.09	0.99
Nature of test–substantive	34.73	0.17	0.14	0.03	0.99
Combination of factors at lowest level	61.48	1.172	0.00	—	—

Overall Model E-9 Summary Statistics

Mean value of dependent variable - sample size judgment 44.86
Coefficient of variation of dependent variable: 1.17
Overall R^2 0.13 F-Statistic 5.10
Adjusted R^2 0.10 Significance 0.01
Improvement in Adjusted R^2 over main effects model: None

Figure 9-4 (continued)

Procedure E-10 (Confirmations)

Model Elements	Model Parameters	Standardized Model Parameters	2-Tail Significance	Contribution to R^2	Tolerance
Nature and timing	152.44	0.30	0.01	0.05	0.60
Experimental treatment	-83.29	-0.27	0.01	0.06	0.80
Experience	-49.10	-0.34	0.00	0.09	0.78
Audit level training	48.65	0.34	0.00	0.07	0.40
Audit test objectives/Experimental treatment	235.29	0.40	0.00	0.03	0.51
Audit test objectives/Nature and timing/ Audit level training	93.85	0.42	0.00	0.08	0.48
Experience/Audit level training	84.85	0.67	0.01	0.05	0.12
Experience/Audit test objectives/Audit level training	-31.34	0.91	0.00	0.10	0.12
Intercept	355.42	2.26	0.00	—	—

Overall Model E-10 Summary Statistics

Mean value of dependent variable - sample size judgment	366.67		
Coefficient of variation of dependent variable:	0.44		
Overall R^2	0.58	F-Statistic	9.68
Adjusted R^2	0.52	Significance	0.00
Improvement in Adjusted R^2 over main effects model:	37%		

Figure 9.4 (continued)

Procedure E-5 (Comparisons)　　　Concurrent Documentation

Model Elements	Model Parameters	Standardized Model Parameters	2-Tail Significance	Contribution to R^2	Tolerance
Nature of test—substantive	-67.91	-0.78	0.02	0.13	0.21
Experimental treatment	-25.82	-0.69	0.11	0.04	0.09
Minimum sample size/Nature of test—substantive	1.14	0.67	0.01	0.09	0.21
Minimum sample size/Experimental treatment	0.47	1.21	0.01	0.14	0.09
Combination of factors at the lowest level	75.11	1.83	0.00	—	—

Overall Model E-5 Summary Statistics

Mean value of dependent variable - sample size judgment	70.91		
Coefficient of variation of dependent variable:	0.58		
Overall R^2	0.57	F-Statistic	8.87
Adjusted R^2	0.50	Significance	0.00
Improvement in Adjusted R^2 over main effects model:	79%		

Figure 9.4 (continued)

Procedure E-6 (Pricing Test)

Model Elements	Model Parameters	Standardized Model Parameters	2-Tail Significance	Contribution to R^2	Tolerance
Maximum sample size	0.09	0.24	0.10	0.04	0.68
Minimum sample size	0.60	0.46	0.00	0.19	0.88
Nature of test–substantive/Maximum sample size	0.25	0.55	0.00	0.17	0.58
Nature of test–substantive/Maximum sample size/ experimental treatment	-0.05	-0.29	0.04	0.06	0.74
Combination of factors at the lowest level	17.29	0.60	0.01	—	—

Overall Model E-6 Summary Statistics

Mean value of dependent variable - sample size judgment   47.78
Coefficient of variation of dependent variable: 0.60
Overall R^2 0.65   F-Statistic   12.37
Adjusted R^2 0.59   Significance   0.00
Improvement in Adjusted R^2 over main effects model: 11%

Figure 9.4 (continued)

Procedure E-9 (Posting Test)

Model Elements	Model Parameters	Standardized Model Parameters	2-Tail Significance	Contribution to R²	Tolerance
Maximum sample size	0.35	0.55	0.00	0.30	0.10
Intercept	14.87	0.28	0.26	—	—

Overall Model E-9 Summary Statistics

Mean value of dependent variable - sample size judgment	51.71		
Coefficient of variation of dependent variable:	1.01		
Overall R²	0.30	F-Statistic	12.75
Adjusted R²	0.27	Significance	0.00
Improvement in Adjusted R² over main effects model:	None		

Figure 9.4 (continued)

Procedure E-10 (Confirmations)

Model Elements	Model Parameters	Standardized Model Parameters	2-Tail Significance	Contribution to R^2	Tolerance
Maximum sample size	0.51	0.44	0.01	0.20	0.99
Materiality	323.13	0.34	0.04	0.11	0.99
Intercept	-120.31	-0.71	0.45	—	—

Overall Model E-10 Summary Statistics

Mean value of dependent variable - sample size judgment	225.96		
Coefficient of variation of dependent variable:	0.68		
Overall R^2	0.28	F-Statistic	5.64
Adjusted R^2	0.23	Significance	0.01
Improvement in Adjusted R^2 over main effects model:	None		

Figure 9.5
Summary of Main Effects Model Parameter (Standardized)
from Figure 9.4 for Retrospective and Concurrent Documentation

	Procedure — Retrospective				Procedure — Concurrent			
	E-5	E-6	E-9	E-10	E-5	E-6	E-9	E-10
Nature and timing	0.28	—	—	0.30	n/a	n/a	n/a	n/a
Other audit evidence	-0.27	—	-0.30	—	n/a	n/a	n/a	n/a
Experimental treatment	-0.27	0.96	—	-0.27	-0.69	—	—	—
Nature of test–substantive	—	0.90	0.17	—	-0.78	—	—	—
Nature of test–compliance	—	0.89	—	—	—	—	—	—
Audit level training	—	—	—	0.34	n/a	n/a	n/a	n/a
Experience	—	—	—	-0.34	n/a	n/a	n/a	n/a
Risk	n/a	n/a	n/a	n/a	—	—	—	0.34
Maximum sample size	n/a	n/a	n/a	n/a	—	0.24	0.55	—
Minimum sample size	n/a	n/a	n/a	n/a	—	0.46	—	0.44

The concurrent documentation task reflected one regression analogue of the ANOVA model, for procedure E-9. The other three procedures E-5, E-6, E-10 all appear to be regression analogues of the ANCOVA model. Tests of the assumptions of the ANCOVA models were negative indicating that these models all have different intercepts and slopes for each level of the quantitatively scaled factors: maximum and minimum sample size judgments. These results will be further discussed in the context of model interpretation which now follows.

MODEL INTERPRETABILITY

The presence of some interaction terms in some of the models, although improving the variance explained and overall fit of the models, does cause some difficulty in explicitly interpreting the effects of the individual model elements.[6] To aid in the interpretation of the various models, the following strategy is employed:

1. Analyze the reduced set of factors through ANOVA techniques, which allow easier computation and comparison of group means for the procedures E-5, and E-6 for the retrospective documentation task.
2. Interpret model E-10 (retrospective), and models E-5, E-6, E-9 and E-10 of the concurrent task using the regression approach to model interpretation.
3. Interpret model E-9 (retrospective) using the ANOVA approach.

The results of these various interpretations are now discussed.

Procedure E-5—Packing Slip/Invoice Comparison— Retrospective Documentation

The model underlying procedure E-5 for the retrospective documentation method is comprised of two significant qualitative factors and five significant interaction terms. The model in notational form is:

$$Y_i = \beta_0 + \beta_1 X_{i1} + \beta_2 X_{i2} + \beta_3 X_{i3}X_{i4} + \beta_4 X_{i3}X_{i1}$$
$$+ \beta_5 X_{i3} + \beta_{i1}X_{i4} + \beta_6 X_{i3}X_{i4} + \beta_7 X_{i1}X_{i2}X_{i4} + \epsilon_i \qquad (9.4)$$

where: Y_i = sample size judgment
β_0 = value of Y when qualitative factors are at the lowest level (zero)
$\beta_{1....7}$ = cue weighting coefficients
X_{i1} = other audit evidence
X_{i2} = experimental treatment
X_{i3} = control reference
X_{i4} = nature and timing of the test

and where i indicates the ith trial

Since there are no quantitative factors, this model does not have a response function. The model interpretation is summarized in figure 9.6.

As noted, several of the "sub-models" above basically are identical with respect to sample size judgments. Other sub-models exhibit wide variability, although the average or overall model does explain 32 percent of the variance. The majority of the auditors seemed to be affected by the experimental control treatment to the relative exclusion of the other factors (note in each case the effect (reduced sample size) is as would be expected). There were, however, enough subjects exhibiting different underlying models to cause the overall model to consist of the combinations of factors presented in figure 9.4.

Procedure E-6—Invoice Pricing Test—Retrospective Documentation

The model underlying procedure E-6 for the retrospective task is the most complex and difficult to explain of all the models discussed in this paper. This complexity is due to the number of significant interaction terms in the model, some of which contain quantitatively-scaled factors interacting with qualitative factors. This model was restricted to main effects and

Figure 9.6
Summary Interpretation of Model E-5 — Retrospective Documentation

Other Audit Evidence (X_1)	Experimental treatment (X_2)	Control Reference (X_3)	Nature and Timing (X_4)	Notational Model	Functional Model: Mean Sample Size Judgment	Number of Auditors for Each Sub-Model	Model Parameter From Figure 9.4
Ref	Strong	Ref	Ref	$E(Y) = \beta_0 + \beta_1 + \beta_2 + \beta_5 + \beta_6 + \beta_7$	10.47	4	$\beta_0 = 78.59$
Ref	Strong	Ref	No Ref	$E(Y) = \beta_0 + \beta_1 + \beta_2 + \beta_4$	76.80	8	$\beta_1 = -16.61$
Ref	Strong	No Ref	Ref	$E(Y) = \beta_0 + \beta_6 + \beta_7$	104.87	4	$\beta_2 = -12.82$
Ref	Strong	No Ref	No Ref	$E(Y) = \beta_0 + \beta_1 + \beta_2$	48.16	1	$\beta_3 = 47.22$
No Ref	Strong	Ref	Ref	$E(Y) = \beta_0 + \beta_2 + \beta_3 + \beta_6$	61.62	1	$\beta_4 = 28.64$
No Ref	Strong	Ref	No Ref	$E(Y) = \beta_0 + \beta_2$	65.77	23	$\beta_5 = -64.97$
No Ref	Strong	No Ref	Ref	$E(Y) = \beta_0 + \beta_2$	65.77	5	$\beta_6 = -51.37$
No Ref	Strong	No Ref	No Ref	$E(Y) = \beta_0 + \beta_2$	65.77	26	$\beta_7 = 77.65$

two-way interactions only, due to the potentially large number of unexplainable higher-order interaction terms. Thus, the overall model may not "explain" as much variance as potentially possible. The model is, however, comparable to the other models for the other procedures in terms of explanatory power and significance, and thus is used in its present form. This model, in notational forms, is represented as:

$$Y_i = \beta_0 + \beta_1 X_{i1} + \beta_2 X_{i2} + \beta_5 \beta_{i4} X_{i5} + \beta_6 X_{i6} X_{i2} + \beta_7 X_{i2} X_{i7}$$
$$+ \beta_8 X_{i2} X_{i1} + \beta_9 X_{i3} X_{i5} + \beta_{10} X_{i3} X_{i1} + \beta_{11} X_{i8} X_{i1} + \epsilon_i \quad (9.5)$$

where:

Y_i	=	sample size judgment
β_0	=	Y value when combined factors are at lowest level
$\beta_1....\beta_{11}$	=	cue weighting coefficients
X_{i1}	=	experimental treatment
X_{i2}	=	nature of the test-substantive
X_{i3}	=	nature of the test-compliance
X_{i4}	=	audit test objectives
X_{i5}	=	audit level training
X_{i6}	=	other audit evidence
X_{i7}	=	nature and timing of the test
X_{i8}	=	compliance test results

and where i indicates the ith trial

The model elements and their relationship for the combination of the factors are not shown in this chapter due to the complexity of the model and difficulty in presenting them. However, in referring to figure 9.4, note that the adjusted $R^2 = 0.49$ and the overall significance of the model is very good.

Procedure E-9—Posting Test—Retrospective Documentation.

The model underlying procedure E-9 for the retrospective documentation is comprised of two qualitative factors as shown in figure 9.4. The resulting model, in notational form is:

$$Y_i = \beta_0 + \beta_{i1}X_{i1} + \beta_2 X_{i2} + \epsilon_i \qquad (9.6)$$

β_0 = value of Y when the qualitative factors are at their lowest level (zero)

β_1, β_2 = cue weighting coefficients

X_{i1} = qualitative factor-other audit evidence

X_{i2} = qualitative factor nature of the test-substantive

and where i indicates the ith trial

Unlike the regression models underlying the concurrent documentation procedures E-5, E-6, and E-9, this regression model does not have a response function or significant interaction terms. Thus, the interpretation of the coefficients of the model is straightforward and is summarized in figure 9.7.

As noted in figure 9.4, reference to other audit evidence results in a mean sample size reduction of 31.51, whereas reference to substantive nature of the test results in a mean sample size increase of 34.73.[7]

Procedure E-10—Accounts Receivable Confirmation— Retrospective Documentation.

The group model underlying procedure E-10 for the retrospective documentation task has two significant qualitative factors, two significant quantitative factors, and four significant interaction terms. The resulting model of figure 9.4 is shown in notational form as:

Figure 9.7
Summary Interpretation of Model E-9 — Retrospective Documentation

Other Audit Evidence (X_1)	Nature of Test-Substantive (X_2)	Notational Model	Functional Model – Mean Sample Judgment	Model Parameters From Figure 9.4
Reference	Reference	$E(Y) = \beta_0 + \beta_1 + \beta_2$	64.70	$\beta_0 = 61.48$
Reference	No Reference	$E(Y) = \beta_0 + \beta_1$	29.97	$\beta_1 = -31.51$
No Reference	Reference	$E(Y) = \beta_0 + \beta_2$	96.21	$\beta_2 = 34.73$
No Reference	No Reference	$E(Y) = \beta_0$	61.48	

$$Y_1 = \beta_0 + \beta_1 X_{i1} + \beta_2 X_{i2} + \beta_3 X_{i3} X_4 + \beta_4 X_{i4}$$
$$+ \beta_5 X_{i5} + \beta_5 X_{i2} + \beta_6 X_{i1} X_{i5} X_{i1} X_{i4}$$
$$+ \beta_7 X_{i3} X_{i4} X_{??} + \beta_8 X_{i5} X_{i3} X_{i4} + \epsilon_i \tag{9.7}$$

where:

Y_i	=	sample size judgment
β_0	=	the intercept term
$\beta_i....\beta_8$	=	cue weighting coefficients
X_{i1}	=	nature and timing of the test
X_{i2}	=	experimental treatment effect
X_{i3}	=	experience as an auditor
X_{i4}	=	audit level training
X_{i5}	=	audit test objectives

and where i indicates the ith trial.[8]

Since there are two quantitatively scaled factors which interact with each other, as well as the qualitative factors, the change in mean sample size judgments is expressed in figure 9.8.[9] As can be seen, each combination of the factors in the model results in a variety of models with different intercepts and slopes. Here, as compared to some of the procedures of the concurrent documentation task, the magnitude of the changes in sample size judgments is quite great. As noted in figure 9.4, the overall model is highly significant and explains a significant amount (adjusted $R^2 = 0.43$) of the variance in auditor judgment.

Procedure E-5—Packing Slip/Invoice Comparison— Concurrent Documentation Task.

The model for procedure E-5 (concurrent documentation) as developed from figure 9.4, has two significant factors and two significant interaction terms. Since both interaction terms contain a quantitatively scaled factor, minimum sample size, the regression model is:

$$Y_i = \beta_0 + \beta_1 X_{i1} + \beta_2 X_{i2} + \beta_3 X_{i3}$$
$$+ \beta_4 X_{i1} X_{i2} + \beta_5 X_{i1} X_{i3} + \epsilon_i \qquad (9.8)$$

where:

Y_i	=	sample size judgment
β_0	=	the intercept term
$\beta_1 .... \beta_5$	=	cue weighting coefficients
X_{i1}	=	minimum sample size[10]
X_{i2}	=	nature of the task-substantive reference
X_{i3}	=	nature of the task-compliance reference
X_{i3}	=	experimental treatment effect

and where i is the ith trial.

This model has different response functions for the different *experimental treatment—nature of the test—substantive* combinations. Also the differential effects of one qualitative factor on the intercept term depend on the particular class of the other qualitative factor. The model elements are summarized in both notational and functional form in figure 9.9.

The functional models imply that minimum sample size appears to serve as an anchor from which to modify sample size judgments based on combinations of the two qualitative factors, internal control and nature of the audit procedure. Here the changes in sample size judgments across different combinations of the referenced factors appear to be substantial.

Procedure E-6—Invoice Pricing Test— Concurrent Documentation

The derived model for procedure E-6 is a regression model with two significant factors and two significant interaction terms. The significant factors in this model are quantitatively-scaled and interact with the two qualitatively-scaled factors.

The model elements are represented in notation form as:

$$Y_i = \beta_0 + \beta_1 X_{i1} + \beta_2 X_{i2} + \beta_3 X_{i3} + \beta_4 X_{i4}$$
$$+ \beta_5 X_{i1} X_{i3} + \beta_6 X_{i1} X_{i2} X_{i3} X_{i4} + \epsilon_i \qquad (9.9)$$

where: Y_i = sample size judgment
β_0 = intercept term
$\beta_1....\beta_6$ = cue weighting coefficients
X_{i1} = maximum sample size
X_{i2} = minimum sample size
X_{i3} = nature of the test-substantive[11]
X_{i4} = experiment treatment effect

and where i indicates the ith trial[12]

Since there are two important quantitatively-scaled factors in the model which interact with each other as well as the two qualitative variables, the *change* in mean sample size judgments is expressed in figure 9.10.

As is noted in figure 9.10, each combination of the factors in the model results in a variety of models with different intercepts and slopes. In this case, the magnitude of the change in the sample size judgments is not very large. This implies that the mean sample size judgment of 75.11 (when all factor levels are zero) is relatively unaffected by the reference (rationale) contained in the concurrent documentation. This, however, does not imply that the derived regression model is not sound. On the contrary, the derived model explains a significant amount (adjusted $R^2 = 0.50$) of the variation in auditor judgment, even though the magnitude of the variation is not great.

Procedure E-9—Posting Test—Concurrent Documentation

As developed from figure 9.4, one factor is present in the simple regression model underlying procedure E-9 (concurrent documentation). This is the ratio-scaled, maximum sample size factor. In notation form, this model is:

Table 9-8
Summary Interpretation of Model E-10 — Retrospective Documentation

Experience (X_3)	Audit Level Training (X_4)	Nature and Audit Test Timing (X_1)	Objectives (X_5)	Treatment (X_2)	Change in Mean Response	Functional Change in Mean Response	Model Parameters From Table 9-4
1 Unit inc	Const.	Ref	Ref	Strong	$\beta_3 + \beta_7 X_5 + \beta_8 X_4 X_5$	$35.41 - 34.35X_4$	$\beta_1 = 152.44$
Constant	Unit inc	Ref	Ref	Strong	$\beta_4 + \beta_6 X_5 X_1 + \beta_7 X_3 + \beta_8 X_3 X_4$	$142.51 + 84.51X_3 - 34.35X_3 X_4$	$\beta_2 = -83.29$
1 Unit inc	Const	Ref	NR	Strong	β_3	-49.10	$\beta_3 = -49.10$
Constant	Unit inc	Ref	NR	Strong	$\beta_4 + \beta_7 X_3 + \beta_8 X_3 X_4$	$48.66 + 84.51X_3 - 34.35X_3 X_4$	$\beta_4 = 48.65$ $\beta_0 = 355.42$ $\beta_5 = 235.29$
1 Unit inc	Const	NR	Ref	Strong	$\beta_3 + \beta_7 + \beta_8 X_4 X_5$	$35.41 - 34.35X_4$	
Constant	Unit inc	NR	NR	Strong	$\beta_4 + \beta_7 X_3 + \beta_8 X_3 X_4$	$48.66 + 84.51X_3 - 34.35X_3 X_4$	$\beta_6 = 93.85$
1 Unit inc	Const	NR	NR	Strong	β_3	-49.10	$\beta_7 = 84.85$
Constant	Unit inc	NR	NR	Strong	$\beta_4 + \beta_7 X_3 + \beta_8 X_3 X_4$	$48.66 + 84.51X_3 - 34.35X_3 X_4$	$\beta_8 = -31.34$

Abbreviation key to above: inc = increase   const = constant
N = No reference   ref = reference

Figure 9.9
Summary Interpretation of Model E-5 — Concurrent Documentation

Experimental Treatment (X_3)	Nature of Test (X_2)	Model Response Function	Functional Model	Model Value From Figure 9.4
Strong	Substantive	$E(Y) = (\beta_0 + \beta_2 + \beta_3) + (\beta_4 + \beta_5)X_1$	$Y = -18.62 + 1.61X_1$	$\beta_5 = -25.80$
Fair	Substantive	$E(Y) = (\beta_0 + \beta_3) + \beta_5 X_1$	$Y = 49.29 + 0.47X_1$	$\beta_5 = -67.91$
Strong	Compliance or Dual	$E(Y) = (\beta_0 + \beta_2) + \beta_4 X_1$	$Y = 7.20 + 1.10X_1$	$\beta_4 = 1.14$ $\beta_5 = 0.47$
Fair	Compliance or Dual	$E(Y) = \beta_0$	$Y = 75.11$	$\beta_0 = 75.11$

$$Y_i = \beta_0 + \beta_1 X_1 + \epsilon_i \qquad (9.10)$$

where: Y_i = sample size judgment
β_0 = the value of Y when X is zero
β_1 = the marginal contribution to Y of a unit increase is X
X_1 = maximum size judgment in the ith trial

The estimated functional form of the model is $Y = 14.87 + 0.35X_1$.

The interpretation of this simple regression model is straight-forward. In effect, this model represents an anchoring and adjustment heuristic (maximum sample size). The marginal change in sample size judgment is 0.35 when the maximum sample size factor is varied by a unit amount. Although the marginal contribution to sample size is not great, the regression model is highly significant ($\alpha = 0.00$) and exhibits an adjusted $R^2 = 0.27$.

Procedure E-10—Accounts Receivable Confirmation Test—Concurrent Documentation

The model underlying procedure E-10 for the concurrent documentation task is comprised of one qualitative and quantitative factor, as shown in figure 9.4. The resulting model, in notational form is:

$$Y_i = \beta_0 + \beta_1 X_{i1} + \beta_2 X_{i2} + \epsilon_i \qquad (9.11)$$

where: Y_i = sample size judgment
β_0 = the value of Y when the factors are at their lowest level
β_1, β_2 = cue weighting coefficients
X_{i1} = minimum sample size judgment
X_{i2} = materiality factor

and where i indicates the ith trial.

This model has a response function with a constant slope and intercept. The interpretation of the model parameters are summarized in figure 9.11.

As noted, since the slope and intercept of the response function are constant, the risk factor indicates how much the sample size judgment

Figure 9.10
Summary Interpretation of Model E-6 — Concurrent Documentation

Condition				Functional Change in Mean Response (Y)	Model Change in Mean Response (Y)	Parameter from Figure
Max Sample Size (X_1)	Min Sample Size (X_2)	Nature of Task (X_3)	Experimental Treatment (X_4)			
9.4						
One unit increase	Held at constant level	Substantive	Strong	$\beta_1 + \beta_5 X_3 + \beta_6 X_2 X_3 X_4$	$0.34 + (-.005)X_2$	$\beta_1 = 0.09$
Held at constant level	One unit increase	Substantive	Strong	$\beta_2 + \beta_6 X_1 X_3 X_4$	$0.60 + (-.005)X_1$	$\beta_2 = 0.60$
One unit increase	Held at constant level	Compliance or Dual	Strong	β_1	0.09	$\beta_5 = 0.25$
One unit increase	Held at constant level	Substantive	Fair	$\beta_1 + \beta_5 X_3$	0.34	$\beta_6 = -0.005$
Held at constant level	One unit increase	Compliance or Dual	Strong	β_2	0.60	$\beta_0 = 75.11$

Mean sample size when all factors are zero: 75.11

Figure 9.11
Summary Interpretation of Model E-10 — Concurrent Documentation

Minimum Sample Size (X_1)	Materiality (X_2)	Notation Model	Functional Model	Model Parameters From Figure 9.4
One unit increase	Material	$E(Y) = (\beta_0 + \beta_2) + \beta_1 X_{i1}$	$202.82 + 51X_1$	$\beta_0 = -120.31$
One unit increase	Immaterial	$E(Y) = \beta_0 + \beta_1 X_{i1}$	$-120.31 + 51X_1$	$\beta_1 = 0.51$ $\beta_2 = 323.13$

changes, given a constant level (anchor) for minimum sample size. The above model is highly significant ($\alpha = 0.01$), although not explaining a great deal of variance, with an adjusted $R^2 = 0.23$.

Model Testing—Predictive Ability

The ultimate assessment of the merit of a regression model is how well it fits new data. To assess the predictive ability of the models, cross validation techniques were employed.

The auditors' data were randomly assigned to two groups so that approximately equal numbers of auditors' data were in each group. One group of data was then used as a basis for developing the model and the second group of data was used as the cross validation set. A goodness-of-fit test based on the F-statistic was used to determine the significance or predictive validity of the model. The F-statistic used is the ratio of the averaged squared residuals for auditors' data within the cross validation set to the residual mean squares for the auditors' data within the model development set.

The cross validation technique was performed for all audit procedures (E-5, E-6, E-9, E-10) over both tasks. The summary results are shown in figure 9.12. As noted there, all models over the two tasks have high predictive ability significance. This implies that the models fitted and presented in figure 9.4, are a reasonably good representation of the data in that they have good ability to fit new data.

Model Representativeness—Nomothetic versus Idiographic

A major premise of this chapter is the nomothetic view that a group model of auditor judgment can be developed and defended. This nomothetic view, in effect, assumes that significant individual differences, if at one time existent, have been mitigated by training or other means. To see how well this assumption holds, several analyses were made on a case by case basis to determine the effects on the judgment models of extreme departures by individual auditors from the group norms.

Figure 9.12

Summary Statistics for Cross-Validation of Models Underlying Four Audit Procedures Over Two Tasks

	Retrospective			
	E-5	E-6	E-9	E-10
F-Statistic	5.96	16.60	2.26	2.61
Significance	0.00	0.00	0.01	0.00
	Concurrent			
F-Statistic	3.01	2.98	2.10	4.89
Significance	0.01	0.01	0.02	0.00

These analyses were directed to evaluating the sensitivity of the regression judgment models to the data for each auditor. These techniques included calculation of the deleted (Press) residuals, Mahalanobia distance, and Cook's distance.[12] The deleted (Press) residual is the residual that would be obtained if an auditor's data were omitted from the computation of the regression. Mahalanobia distance is the distance of each auditor's data from the mean of all auditors' data used to estimate the regression equation—a large distance indicates that the case is an outlier in the space defined by the factors. Cook's distance is a measure of the change in the coefficient of the regression that would occur if the auditor's data were omitted from the computation of the coefficients.

Cook's distance incorporates the deleted (Press) residual and Mahalanobia distance statistics as follows:

$$\text{Cook's Distance} = \frac{r^2 v}{(p+1)\text{RMS}} \tag{9.12}$$

where r denotes the deleted (Press) residual, where the term $(p+1)$ is dropped if the intercept is zero, RMS denotes residual mean square.

Partial results of these analyses are presented in figure 9.13. As noted there, in most cases the relative magnitude and signs of the coefficients remain fairly consistent. There are, however, some exceptions where outliers in the data cause serious changes in the coefficients, e.g., the change of some of the interaction coefficients in E-10 (retrospective).

Figure 9.13
Comparison of Estimates of Regression Coefficients
When Considering Cases with Largest
Cook's Distance (Partial Results)

Retrospective

Proc.	Model Element	Model Parameters From Figure 9.4	Model Parameters Omitting Case with Largest Cook's Distance	Relative % Difference
E-9	OAE	-31.51	-28.47	10
	NTS	34.73	9.14	74
	INT	61.48	59.60	3
E-10	INT	355.42	339.53	4
	TRT	-83.29	-80.88	3
	NT	152.44	156.27	4
	ALT	48.66	51.09	5
	ATO/NT/ALT	93.85	82.57	12
	EXP/ATO	84.52	892.15	956
	EXP/ATO/ALT	-31.35	-230.22	634
	EXP	-49.10	-47.67	3
	ATO/TRT	235.29	66.90	72

Figure 9.13 (continued)

Concurrent

Proc.	Model Element	Model Parameters From Figure 9.4	Model Parameters Omitting Case with Largest Cook's Distance	Relative % Difference
E-5	TRT	-25.82	-30.53	-20
	NTS	-67.91	-63.44	7
	MISS/NTS	1.14	1.18	-4
	MISS/TRT	0.47	0.51	-10
	INT	75.11	75.58	-2
E-6	MASS	.09	.01	89
	MISS	.60	.69	-16
	NTS/MASS	.26	.32	-25
	NTS/MISS/ MASS/TRT	-.005	-.006	-12
	INT	17.29	17.43	-1

Key to abbreviations:

  OAE = Other audit evidence

  TRT = Experimental treatment

    CR = General and specific control reference

    NT = Nature and timing of test

   INT = Intercept of the model

  NTS = Nature of the test - Substantive

  NTC = Nature of the test - Compliance

  ATO = Audit test objective

  ALT = Audit level training courses completed

  CTR = Compliance test results

  EXP = Years of audit experience

 MISS = Minimum sample size

MASS = Maximum sample size

These outliers were not removed from the models presented in figure 9.4 since they represented valid representations of individual auditors in the experimental procedures and were not error in the data. The presence of these outliers, where their presence causes serious changes in the coefficients, gives some cause for questioning the complete satisfaction of the nomothetic model assumption. Although not reported in this paper, it was noted during the analysis that the subjects who exhibited "non-normal" behavior in a given procedure such as E-10 (retrospective) exhibited "normal" behavior in other audit procedures.

In general, the lack of homogeneity in aggregate or group model building research should not be troublesome as long as general group tendencies of individual subjects are noted. In the current research, with minor exceptions, the nomothetic model assumption seems to be reasonable and adequately reflects the data. Another evidence of this conclusion is the high predictive ability of all the models even when some of the coefficients of some models may vary in presence of "non-normal" auditor behavior.

Documentation Effects

Research question six is concerned with a comparison of the two groups of tasks models, that is, the retrospective documentation models versus the concurrent documentation models. Recall that, the concurrent documentation task consisted of structured documentation judgments, whereas the retrospective documentation task consisted of open-ended, rationale memos developed after the judgments were made. The main difference between these two documentation tasks was one of timing. The question of interest now is which of the two types of documentation provides the better models in context of overall variance explained in auditor judgment.

Since the model elements are somewhat different for the two types of models, the typical methods of comparing regression models cannot be utilized. Rather, a more subjective appraisal is made based on looking at general model statistics for the two types of models. These statistics include Adjusted R^2, Residual Mean Squares, and Standard Error of the Estimate. The results of these statistics are summarized in figure 9.14.

As noted in figure 9.14, the concurrent documentation models appear to be superior to the retrospective documentation models for all audit procedures except for E-10. The models for procedure E-10 support the retrospective task as being superior. One explanation for this is that the three procedures, E-5, E-6 and E-9, are by their nature more structured, and perhaps require more specific reliance on or reference to specific kinds of documentation. On the other hand, procedure E-10 is concerned with confirmation of accounts receivable and thus, by nature this procedure may be more general and thus capture the more general kinds of control reference demonstrated in the models of figure 9.4.

DISCUSSION OF RESULTS

The analytical results presented in the previous sections are addressed to two general research issues. Research questions 1 through 5 address the significant amount of auditor judgment variability which was not "explained" by the experimental treatments using the largely univariate analysis presented in chapters 7 and 8. Research question 6 is concerned with the comparative "value" of two methods of documenting auditor judgment.

Unexplained Variability

Using statistical methods based on the general linear model, the first five research questions were addressed to derive improved descriptive models of auditor judgment. In comparison to the variance explained by experimental treatments alone, models based upon data developed from both concurrent and retrospective documentation were derived which exhibited greater explained variance (adjusted R^2s). In addition to explaining more variance, these models were found to be robust both with respect to predictive validity, and various residual analyses.

Although some evidence of individual specific (idiosyncratic) behavior was obtained, general (nomotheric) models were found to describe a substantial amount of the observed variance in auditor judgments.

Figure 9.14

Summary of Statistics to Compare Retrospective (Retro)
versus Concurrent (Conc) Documentation Models
Over Four Procedures

Statistics	E-5		E-6		E-9		E-10	
	Retro	Conc	Retro	Conc	Retro	Conc	Retro	Conc
Adjusted R^2 Residual	0.32	0.50	0.49	0.59	0.10	0.27	0.52	0.23
Mean square	2458	838	985	337	2,472	1,996	11,911	22,312
Standard error of the Estimate	50	29	31	18	50	45	109	147
Best model in terms of above three criteria (X)		X		X		X	X	

A previous section presented the various models in detail including a discussion of the functional form of the models, the contribution of each factor, and the signs and weights of included variables. In general, these models were found to be quite complex with several models containing significant interaction terms. In most cases the included variables and their direction of impact were as expected. For example, reliance on other audit evidence was negatively related to sample size recommendations. In only one case did the addition of training or other demographic variables result in a significant increase in explained variance (as a main effect). On the other hand, several variables, such as cost and risk considerations, which may have been expected to appear in the models, did not appear.

The derived judgment models for all audit procedures given concurrent documentation, may be interpreted as anchoring and adjustment heuristics based on either a minimum or maximum sample size judgment.[13]

All results taken into consideration, the combined approach of the multiple research methodologies utilized in other chapters within this Anthology and the multivariate statistical methods applied in this chpater have led to improved descriptive models of audit sample size judgments.

Comparative "Value" of the Documentation Methods

Previous analyses in chapter 8 have shown that when documentation method was an experimental variable in an ANOVA model, no significant difference in the recommendations analyzed here were observed. This left open the question of whether one method of documenting auditing judgments was better than another from either a research or audit review perspective. Although both the open-ended (retrospective) and structured (concurrent) methods were found lacking in comprehensiveness in chapter 8, careful study and coding of the documentation produced by both methods led to models with statistically high descriptive and predictive characteristics. In the cases of the transaction cycle audit procedures (E-5, E-6 and E-9), the structured, concurrent method produced a greater amount of explained variance. In the case of a test of account balances, the open-ended, retrospective method led to higher explained variance. Whether the two approaches differ in terms of cost of coding and analysis or produce models which are generally descriptive of auditor behavior is the subject of future research.

SUMMARY

Prior chapters have presented results of initial analysis using primarily univariate methodologies. After univariate analyses, however, a substantial degree of variance in both subject-recommended sample sizes and related coefficients of variation remains unexplained. Using statistical methods based on the general linear model, this chapter has presented improved descriptive models of auditor judgment by introducing the previously unexamined issue of adequacy of auditor judgment documentation. To accomplish this, two different forms of auditor rationale memos, concurrent and retrospective, generated during the field experiment were used to build improved models of auditor judgments. Concurrent documentation was in a structured format while retrospective documentation was open-ended. A summary of the results for each identified research question is as follows:

Research Question 1: What is the nature of the decision (judgment) models underlying sample size judgments based on concurrent and retrospective documentation techniques?

Outcome: In general, the models were found to be quite complex with several models containing significant interaction terms. In comparison to the variance explained by experimental treatments alone, models based upon data developed from both concurrent and retrospective documentation were derived which exhibited greater explained variance (adjusted R^2 s). In addition to explaining more variance, these models were found to be robust both with respect to predictive validity and various residual analyses. The derived judgment models for all audit procedures given concurrent documentation, may be interpreted as anchoring and adjustment heuristics based on either a minimum or maximum sample size judgment.

Research Question 2: What is the relative importance of the various factors in the models?

Outcome: In most cases the included variables and their direction of impact were as expected. For example, reliance on other audit evidence was negatively related to sample size recommendations. In only one case did the addition of training or other demographic variables result in a significant increase in explained variance (as a main effect). On the other hand, several variables which may have been expected to appear in the models (e.g. cost and risk considerations) did not appear.

Research Question 3: Are the derived cue weights assigned to the various factors stable across audit procedures?

Outcome: In most cases the relative magnitude and signs of the coefficients remain fairly consistent. There are, however, some exceptions where outliers in the data cause serious changes in the coefficients.

Research Question 4: Do the descriptive, derived models have predictive validity?

Outcome: The auditors' data were randomly assigned to two groups so that approximately equal numbers of auditors' data were in each group. One group of data was then used as a basis for developing the model and the second group of data was used as the cross validation set. A goodness-of-fit test based on the F-statistic was used to determine the significance or predictive validity of the model. The F-statistic used is the ratio of the averaged squared residuals for auditors' data within the cross validation set to the residual mean squares for the auditors' data within the model development set.   The cross validation technique was performed for all four audit procedures over both tasks. All models over the two tasks have high predictive ability significance. This implies that the models fitted are a reasonably good representation of the data in that they have good ability to fit new data.

Research Question 5: What are the effects of individual auditor differences on the model parameters?

Outcome: Although some evidence of individual specific (idiosyncratic) behavior was obtained, general (nomotheric) models were found to describe a substantial amount of the observed variance in auditor judgments.

Research Question 6: Are there significant differences between the concurrent documentation and the retrospective documentation models? If so, what is the basis of similarities/ dissimilarities in the two models?

Outcome: Coding of the documentation produced by both methods led to models with statistically high descriptive and predictive characteristics. For the three audit program procedures related to the transaction cycle, the structured, concurrent method produced a greater amount of explained variance. For the fourth audit program procedure testing account balances, the open-ended retrospective method resulted in higher explained variance.

NOTES

1. The chapter is based on T.J. Mock and P.R. Watkins, (1983), presented at the fourth biennial Symposium on Auditing Research, University of Illinois, November 13-14, 1980.

2. M.W. Wartofsky, *Conceptual Foundations of Scientific Thought*, (New York: MacMillan Co., 1968)

3. For a summary, see G.F. Klersey and T.J. Mock, "Verbal Protocol Research in Auditing," *Accounting, Organizations, and Society* 14 (1989): 133.

4. Best was defined in terms of Mallows' Cp [C. Daniel and F. S. Wood, *Fitting Equations To Data* (New York: Wiley, 1980)]:

$$Cp = \frac{RSS}{s^{2-(N-2p')}} \qquad (9.14)$$

where RSS is the residue sums of squares for the best subset being tested, p' is the number of factors in the subset (including the intercept, if any), s^2 is the residual mean square based on the regression using all independent variables. Best is defined as the smallest Cp. The t-statistics for the coefficients of the factors for the subset that minimizes Cp tend to be greater than 2.0 in absolute value. In the language of stepwise regression, the subset that minimized Cp is such that the F-to-remove value for variables in the subset tend to be greater than 2.0 and the F-to-enter values for the remaining variables tend to be less than 2.0.

5. In studies such as this where there are a large number of non-orthogonal independent variables (factor) multicollinearity among the independent variables is common. This creates a problem in that the model elements and predictive ability of the model are unstable. Tolerance is a measure of the degree of multicollinearity of a given factor with all other factors (independent variable) in the model. Tolerance values approaching 1 indicate no multicollinearity. And values approaching zero indicate high multicollinearity.

6. In an attempt to make important interactions unimportant, several transformations of the dependent variables (sample size judgments) were undertaken. These included log, square root and squared transformations. Although removing some important interactions and making them unimportant, the transformation allowed additional interaction terms to enter the model. In the case of the squared transformation, all models showed significant improvements in R^2 but at the sacrifice of interpretability. Hence, these transformed results are not reported.

7. These sample size increases are reported here as point estimates. For completeness these should have confidence intervals placed around them using the Bonferroni interval.

8. Note that this is the only model containing demographics as main effects.

9. The change in mean response is used here and for Procedure E-6 (concurrent) for simplicity in representing the more complex, interactions of the various submodels. The *change* function is a partial derivative of the overall model based on the quantitative factor held constant in the model.

10. This factor was not significant in the overall model independently.

11. These terms were not significant in the model but do appear in interaction terms and hence are included for completeness.

12. R.D. Cook, "Detection of Influential Observations in Linear Regression." *Technometrics* 19 (1977): 15-18.

13. Given that some audit firms have established minimum sample size standards for certain audit circumstances, such standards can influence the risk of unwarranted reliance and of undetected errors and irregularities.

CHAPTER 10

Experimental Results: Auditors' Rationale and Modeling of Audit Decision Process

This chapter considers the content of the auditor's rationale memos and the possible effect of experimentally controlled variables on them. The research technique of content analysis provides a summary of the factors that auditors documented as being important determinants of their decisions. The possibility exists, of course, that these documented factors were not important determinants of their behavior and that they lacked self-insight.[1] The memos are analyzed from a number of perspectives, including self-insight, comprehensiveness, and evidence of auditor heuristics.

The documentation of the various steps and important judgments of the audit process is important for day-to-day review, for the development of quality control reviews of performance and for assessing compliance with designated standards. Often this documentation is in the form of rationale memos that describe the auditor's underlying logic at each phase of the audit. Such rationale memos were collected as part of the subject's requirements in completing the Olde Oak case.

CONTENT ANALYSIS OF AUDITORS' RATIONALE MEMOS

In these experiments, content analysis was applied to the rationale memos for each audit procedure for all subjects except the structured-guidance subjects. These subjects did not prepare rationale memos; rather, they completed a structured planning memo, as detailed in chapter 7. The results of this study phase are presented after a brief discussion of methodology. Methodological issues include the development of a dictionary of themes within which to classify the rationale and the reliability and validity of the classification process.

Methodology

According to Berelson's definition, a content analysis may use any of five different types of units to code data: words, themes, characters, items, and space-and-time measures.[2] Of these types, analysis using words or themes seemed most applicable to rationale memos. The word is probably the basic unit of analysis in most content studies, particularly with the emergence of computer-based content analysis. However, since this study is concerned with references to particular audit cues, it is well suited to thematic analysis. An early attempt was made to use words as the coding units, but this approach was abandoned because it did not capture the audit rationale realistically. Themes were a natural outgrowth of the cues.

A theme is a subject or a topic of discourse, such as a sentence or proposition about something. Thematic analysis is more complex than analyses employing other types of units. First, it is often quite difficult to discern the boundaries between themes. This is true because physical evidence of boundaries is not present as it is with words, sentences, or paragraphs. In addition, several themes may coexist within one sentence, which makes analysis all the more difficult.

The development of themes in this study was accomplished through an iterative process. First, a preliminary dictionary of themes was prepared, and the no-guidance and narrative-guidance rationale memos were scored jointly by the researchers.[3] This process led to a first revision of the dictionary and the related set of theme definitions.

Each researcher independently used the revised dictionary to code the rationale memos derived from the statistical approach experiment. Reconciliation of the coding resulted in only a few minor changes in the dictionary of themes. A summary of theme categories is presented in figure 10.1. The formal definitions used in the coding are included in figure 10.2. This finalized set of themes and definitions was used to code both the statistical approach and the manager review memos and to code a random sample of twenty memos each from the no-guidance and narrative-guidance experiments.

Figures 10.3 and 10.4 contain the final results of the content analysis. These results will be presented after a discussion of the measurement, reliability, and validity of the coding (content analysis) process.

Measurement

The themes used in content analysis can be quantified in several ways. Assigning numbers to the objects of content analysis through nominal measurement is the most useful method. After categorization of units, the frequency of observations in each category is counted. The frequencies thus indicate the raw number of times a theme such as "audit procedure objective" appeared in the rationale memos. As such, the frequencies incorporate a limitation of double (or multiple) counting if one auditor referenced the same theme more than once. Thus, a second measurement, labeled comprehensiveness, is provided in figures 10.4 and 10.5. Comprehensiveness measures the percentage of subjects who referenced each theme (cue) one or more times and thus eliminates double counting.

Figure 10.1
Summary of Categories of Themes
Used in Content Analysis

Category Number	Brief Description
1	Test objective
2	Audit risk in account, item being audited
3	Referred controls or strengths
4	Compliance test results
5	Amount of reliance placed on control(s)
6	Nature of population
7	Cost or benefit factors
8	Other cues relied upon
9	Specification of alternate or complementary audit procedures
10	Statistical reasoning or rationale
11	Heuristic reasoning (rules of thumb)
12	Evaluation of planned sample size

Figure 10.2
Content Analysis Dictionary

Category 1: Test Objective
Reference to nature of test (e.g., substantive test, compliance test, dual test)
Examples of possible objectives:
- Validity of recorded transactions.
- Proper authorization of transactions (balance).
- Assignment of proper initial economic value for recording purposes.
- Accurate recording of transactions.
- Proper valuation of transactions to reflect current economic value.

Category 2: Audit Risk in Account, Item Being Audited
Some mention of audit risk (e.g., possibility of error, understatement, overstatement), error type(e.g. goods billed do not correspond to goods shipped, accuracy, missing invoices, shipments with no corresponding billing), materiality.

Category 3: Reference to General or Specific Controls and Strengths
Reference to evaluation of general controls (e.g., "controls are strong"). Reference to specific controls or strengths:
- S-1 Prenumbered sales invoices are prepared for all sales, issued sequentially, and numerically accounted for.
- S-2 After sales invoices are initialed, one copy is kept in the numerical suspense file until other copies of the invoice are returned from the warehouse.
- S-3 Sales invoices are required for warehouse personnel to fill an order.
- S-4 The dispatcher matches the corrected sales invoice with the packing slip of the merchandise shipped.
- S-5 The general office clerk matches copies 1 and 2 of the sales invoices received from the dispatcher with the control copy 3. The numerical suspense file is periodically reviewed for undelivered orders.
- S-6 Sales invoice customer suspense file reviewed monthly for unmatched invoices.
- S-7 An independent clerk checks pricing of invoice items and also checks extensions and footing.
- S-8 The manager reviews monthly statements and attached invoices and spot checks some of the aged trial balances.
- US-1 The dispatcher maintains an independent numerical packing slip file (note that this control was not identified as a strength in the case).

Category 4: Compliance Test Results
Some mention of the results of completed compliance tests (e.g., no exceptions were noted).

Audit Procedure	Control Strength Tested	Results
Ea, b	S-1	As a result of a management letter comment, the clerks have been issuing invoices on a strict numerical sequence. The audit test revealed no exceptions to this control strength.

| E-7 | S-6 | The clerk assigned the responsibility of reviewing the customer suspense file monthly was still not following up on unmatched invoices (step E-7). |

Audit Procedure	Control Strength Tested	Results
E-6a	S-7	The compliance test for the clerk's initials indicating checking of prices, extensions, and footings (step E-6a) failed on the 33rd item tested.
E-8	S-8	Step E-8 revealed that the manager was still performing only a limited review and spot check of the monthly statements, invoices, and aged trial balance.

Category 5: Amount of Reliance Placed on Control(s)
Some statement about the amount of reliance placed on controls (e.g., significant, some, none).

Category 6: Nature of Population
Statement about the nature of the population (invoices for E-5, E-6, E-9; receivables for E-10) (e.g., variability of dollar units, expected error frequency, or expected error magnitude.)

Category 7: Cost or Benefit Factors
Some statement about cost or benefit factors of the procedure or the evidence generated (e.g., it would combine with another step, the procedure gives limited results, the step is justified, it enables us to limit the confirmation effort, time could be better used, it does not serve a useful purpose).

Category 8: Other Cues Relied Upon
For example, confirmation replies, analytical review of cost of goods sold, substantive test in the previous year, the fact that last year 150 was determined to be an adequate sample size, firm literature on judgement samples.

Statement about the influence of other audit evidence on the sample size decision:
- Reference to last year's results.
- Other evidence that has been or may be collected this year.

Category 9: Alternative or Complimentary Audit Procedure
Statement about the need to add a new audit procedure to the program or to substitute for the procedure being evaluated.

Category 10: Statistical Reasoning or Rationale
For example, statistical sampling or an attribute sampling rationale.

Category 11: Heuristic Reasoning
Some reference to a rule of thumb or heuristic rationale used to reach or justify a decision (e.g., 10 percent confirmation is "normal").

<u>Category 12: Evaluation of Planned Sample Size</u>
Some statement about the adequacy or inadequacy of previously planned sample size (e.g., it is large, excessive, adequate, inadequate, or too small).

Pitfalls in Content Analysis and Reliability
and Validity Considerations

Although content analysis can be quite useful in analyzing data (a text) that would otherwise be difficult to interpret, it still has some pitfalls. The link between thinking and the ability to report accurately on those factors that influence decisions is somewhat tenuous. For example, Nisbett and Wilson described a series of experiments related to retrospective reports on mental processes.[4] Their findings pointed to the difficulty in accurately reporting on the factors that affect perceptions.

The classification of items can also cause a deficiency in a study. Since the researcher decides on the categories and classification of items, the results can be biased by a researcher's decisions. To minimize this deficiency, categories could be selected prior to the research from data not being used in the study. Also, a second researcher should independently classify themes as a means of checking reliability.

To lend credibility to these findings, attention was paid to intercoder reliability. Intercoder reliability, as used in this study, is a measure of the independent coders' agreement on the specific assignment of these categories, taking chance agreement into account. A coefficient of agreement for nominal scales (developed by Cohen) was used to determine reliability between coders.[5] Tests for intercoder reliability revealed that there was a statistically significant level of agreement between coders for each set of rationale memos. The results for the forty randomly selected memos from the no-guidance and narrative-guidance experiments are summarized in figure 10.3. Reliability ranged from 50 percent to 62 percent, which, although not high, seems reasonable, given the fourteen theme categories used. Reconciled coding, which is used in subsequent analysis, resulted in 95 percent to 100 percent agreement.

It is difficult to assess the validity of a classification scheme such as the one used here. It does exhibit face validity, since the themes are those used by auditors in their rationale memos. In addition, they compare quite closely with those developed independently by Roberts .[6]

Figure 10.3
Reliability Results for Content Analysis of 40 Randomly Selected Rationale Memos
From the No-Guidance and Narrative-Guidance Experiments

| | Audit Procedure | | | |
	E-5 Packing Slip Comparison	E-6 Pricing Test	E-9 Posting Test	E-10 Confirmations
Initial agreement memo	59%	57%	67%	56%
Cohen's kappa measure (adjusts for chance agreement)	54%	54%	62%	50%
Ultimate agreement ratio after reconciliation of differences	100%	100%	95%	98%
Z score (all significant at $\alpha \leq .10$)	16.7	6.0	5.5	5.9

Content Analysis Results

The frequency and comprehensiveness scores for each audit procedure and for each experiment except the structured documentation are shown in figures 10.4 and 10.5. A brief review of these figures shows that the subjects were not particularly comprehensive in their memos and that the subjects exhibited a great deal of variability in the contents of their rationales. Lack of comprehensiveness is indicated because only a few themes were referenced by more than 50 percent of the subjects in their rationales. Only two items were mentioned by a majority of auditors over 50 percent of the time: compliance test results and other cues relied upon. Some items that would seem to be important in the review process were mentioned rather infrequently: the objective of the audit procedure, the risk (exposure) inherent in the transaction/account being audited, and the reliance being placed on controls. Clearly, these are items that auditors do consider; thus, their lack of explicit inclusion in the memos may be a result of such factors as lack of time or lack of guidance in memo preparation. Other possible factors are discussed by Ericsson and Simon.[7]

One question that may be partially answered by these data is the effect of the indirect guidance that was provided in the narrative-guidance, statistical-approach, and manager-review experiments. To evaluate this effect statistically, the comprehensiveness scores were aggregated and averaged by audit procedure for each experiment and for all procedures (figure 10.6). The overall aggregation was calculated for both the first twelve themes (excluding counting the sample size recommendation) and the first nine themes (excluding counting statistical and heuristic reasoning and discussion (anchoring) of the planned samples). Figure 10.6 shows that, on the average, subjects referenced about one-third of the items. However, the guidance provided in the statistical-approach and the manager-review experiments increased the comprehensiveness scores for both the twelve- and nine-theme analyses. Analysis of variance applied to these scores indicated statistically significant differences.

In addition to providing some evidence on the comprehensiveness of rationale and the effect of guidance, the content analysis provides some limited evidence about auditors' self-insight. In psychological and decision-making literature, self-insight indicates the ability of an expert decision maker to explicate the factors (cues or themes) that affected his or her decision. For example, did the auditors who indicated they were relying on other audit evidence (theme 9) reduce the extent of their testing? Figure 10.7 summarizes the results of an analysis of variance of such subjects, with the hypothesis being that subjects who indicated reliance would have recommended smaller samples. Although categorizing subjects in this way did not result in explaining a statistically significant amount of variance, in each case the difference was in the expected direction. Analysis of other theme categories also resulted in no significant sample size effects.

Finally, the content analysis data provide some evidence about the existence of anchoring among the subjects. The theme "evaluation of planned sample" indicates an explicit evaluation of the planned sample sizes within subjects' rationale memos. In approximately 10 percent of the cases, subjects explicitly evaluated the planned sample within their rationale memos.

SUMMARY

This chapter has presented the results of the content analysis of subjects' rationale memos. The following chapter presents a related analysis, a protocol study of the subjects' information search and sample size choice processes. Rationale memo content was found:

(1) to be significantly affected by the guidance treatments,

(2) to vary considerably among auditors, and

(3) to exhibit limited comprehensiveness.

As will be seen, the protocol study indicates up to 88 percent comprehensiveness in subjects' information search of the provided audit materials. Thus, although the subjects attended to a large percentage of the audit materials, a very small proportion of the possible relevant factors ended up in their rationale memos.

Figure 10.4
Summary of Content Analysis of Combined No-Guidance and Narrative-Guidance Subjects

Audit Procedure	Content Measure*	Test Objective	Audit Risk	Internal Control Reference	Compliance Test Results	Reliance Placed on Controls	Nature of Population	Cost or Benefit	Other Cues Relied Upon	Complete-Audit Procedures Specified	Statistical Reasoning	Heuristic Reasoning	Evaluation of Planned Sample
No Guidance													
E-5: Packing slip comparison	Frequency	5	1	2	7	0	1	6	7	10	2	0	2
	Comprehensiveness	.60	.10	.20	.50	0	.10	.50	.50	.70	.20	0	.20
E-6: Pricing test	Frequency	6	1	2	9	8	1	4	3	6	4	0	1
	Comprehensiveness	.50	.10	.20	.70	.60	.10	.30	.20	.40	.40	0	.10
E-9: Posting	Frequency	3	0	0	6	0	0	4	4	9	0	1	1
	Comprehensiveness	.20	.10	0	.50	0	0	.30	.40	.60	0	.10	.10
E-10: Confirmations	Frequency	2	1	1	5	2	3	7	9	4	0	12	7
	Comprehensiveness	.20	.10	.10	.30	.20	.30	.60	.80	.30	0	.70	.70

Audit Procedure	Content Measure*	Test Objective	Audit Risk	Internal Control Reference	Compliance Test Results	Reliance Placed on Controls	Nature of Population	Cost or Benefit	Other Cues Relied Upon	Complete Audit Procedures Specified	Statistical Reasoning	Heuristic Reasoning	Evaluation of Planned Sample
Narrative Guidance													
E-5: Packing slip comparison	Frequency	7	4	9	14	1	0	5	13	3	1	1	1
	Comprehensiveness	.30	.20	.60	.90	.10	0	.40	.40	.20	.10	.10	.10
E-6: Pricing test	Frequency	7	1	2	6	3	0	5	5	9	5	0	0
	Comprehensiveness	.40	0	.20	.60	.30	0	.30	.40	.40	.20	0	0
E-9: Posting	Frequency	4	3	1	5	1	0	5	6	3	0	0	0
	Comprehensiveness	.40	.20	.10	.50	.10	0	.60	.60	.30	0	0	0
E-10: Confirmations	Frequency	1	1	1	8	2	0	4	16	4	0	5	2
	Comprehensiveness	.10	.10	.10	.80	.20	0	.30	.80	.20	0	.30	.20

Note: N = 20 randomly selected memos from each experiment

* *Frequency* measures the total number of times a theme was used with replications counted.
Comprehensiveness measures percent of auditors who utilized each theme category at least once in their rationale memos.

Figure 10.5
Summary of Content Analysis Results of Statistical Approach and Manager Review

Audit Procedure	Content Measure*	Test Objec- tive	Audit Risk	Internal Control Refer- ence	Compli- ance Test Results	Reliance Placed on Controls	Nature of Popu- lation	Cost or Benefit	Other Cues Relied Upon	Comple- te Audit Procedures Specified	Sta- tistical Rea- soning	Heuristic Rea- soning	Evalua- tion of Planned Sample
Statistical Approach													
E-5: Packing slip comparison	Frequency	27	16	19	17	6	12	30	39	13	14	2	4
	Comprehen- siveness	.73	.30	.43	.43	.13	.30	.60	.67	.33	.43	.07	.13
E-6: Pricing test	Frequency	14	9	16	19	6	6	29	33	10	26	0	4
	Comprehen- siveness	.50	.31	.50	.62	.23	.19	.77	.69	.35	.77	0	.15
E-9: Posting	Frequency	16	10	14	18	4	5	27	30	14	7	2	3
	Comprehen- siveness	.48	.33	.37	.37	.15	.19	.70	.63	.22	.26	.07	.11
E-10: Confirm- mations	Frequency	1	18	2	22	19	15	19	46	17	n/a	13	2
	Comprehen- siveness	.04	.46	.07	.68	.61	.43	.43	.82	.43	n/a	.39	.07

Figure 10.6

Average Cue Comprehensiveness Scores Classified According to
Audit Procedure and Treatment and Results of Variance Analysis

Audit Procedure	Treatment			F-test
	No Guidance	Narrative Guidance	Statistical Approach	Manager Review	(Significant at $\alpha \leq .10$?)
E-5: Packing slip comparison	.30	.28	.38	.36	No
E-6: Pricing test	.30	.23	.42	.36	No
E-9: Posting test	.19	.23	.32	.27	No
E-10: Confirmations	.36	.26	.45	.37	No
Aggregated over all procedures (12 themes)	.29	.25	.39	.34	Yes
Aggregated over all procedures (9 themes)	.31	.31	.43	.39	Yes

Manager Review

Audit Procedure	Content Measure*	Test Objective	Audit Risk	Internal Control Reference	Compliance Test Results	Reliance Placed on Controls	Nature of Population	Cost or Benefit	Other Cues Relied Upon	Complete Audit Procedures Specified	Statistical Reasoning	Heuristic Reasoning	Evaluation of Planned Sample
E-5: Packing slip comparison	Frequency	12	10	23	36	6	12	13	48	6	4	3	5
	Comprehensiveness	.37	.30	.47	.67	.23	.30	.40	.73	.23	.20	.17	.20
E-6: Pricing test	Frequency	11	10	23	23	11	2	14	35	0	4	0	0
	Comprehensiveness	.30	.33	.53	.67	.33	.07	.43	.63	.30	.57	0	.13
E-9: Posting	Frequency	7	4	30	26	4	5	16	25	1	3	0	0
	Comprehensiveness	.24	.14	.59	.62	.14	.14	.45	.48	.10	.17	.03	.10
E-10: Confirmations	Frequency	4	19	12	24	4	25	22	63	13	9	0	0
	Comprehensiveness	.13	.50	.30	.67	.13	.53	.50	.93	.03	.03	.33	.30

Note: N = all rationale memos.

* *Frequency* measures the total number of times a theme was used with replications counted.
Comprehensiveness measures percent of auditors who utilized each theme category at least once in their rationale memos.

Figure 10.7
Auditors' Self-Insight Analyzed in Terms of Effects of
Explicit Reliance References on Sample Size Decisions for
Combined No-Guidance and Narrative-Guidance Experiments

Audit Procedure	Independent Variable	Classification	Group Sample Size Means	F Value	Significant at α ≤ .10?
E-5: Packing slip comparison	Relied on other audit evidence?	Yes No	81.7 82.3	.001	No
E-6: Pricing test	Relied on other audit evidence?	Yes No	66.7 74.8	.54	No
E-9: Posting test	Relied on other audit evidence?	Yes No	57.7 73.3	1.30	No
E-10: Confirmations	Relied on other audit evidence?	Yes No	328 385	2.65	No

A summary of the hypothesis test results related to this chapter is as follows:

Hypothesis	Results
H7 - Guidance Effects	Significantly different comprehensiveness scores for two treatments

H7: Guidance Effects. The content of rationale memos is expected to vary according to the type and explicitness of guidance provided.

One-way ANOVA results indicate that guidance provided in the statistical-approach and the manager-review experiments significantly increased the comprehensiveness scores for both the twelve-theme and the nine-theme analyses.

NOTES

1. Lack of self-insight has been observed in a number of psychological studies of expert decision makers.

2. Bernard Berelson, "Content Analysis, "in *Handbook of Social Psychology,* ed. Gardner Lindzey, vol. 1 (Cambridge, Mass.: Addison-Wesley Publishing Co., 1954), pp. 488-522.

3. The results of the initial coding and related dictionary are contained in Theodore J. Mock and Jerry L. Turner, "The Effect of Changes in Internal Controls on Audit Programs," *Behavioral Experiments in Accounting II,* ed. Thomas J. Burns (Columbus: The Ohio State University, 1979), pp. 277-326.

4. Richard E. Nisbett and Timothy Decamp Wilson, "Telling More Than We Can Know: Verbal Reports on Mental Processes," *Psychological Review* 84 (May 1977): 231-59; and K. Anders Ericsson and Herbert A Simon, *Retrospective Verbal Reports as Data,* Complex

Information Processing Working Paper 388, and *Thinking-Aloud Protocols as Data: Effects of Verbalization,* Complex Information Processing Working Paper 397 (Pittsburgh: Carnegie Mellon University, 1978 and 1979).

5. Jacob Cohen, "A Coefficient of Agreement for Nominal Scales," *Educational and Psychological Measurement* 20 (Spring 1960): 37-46.

6. Donald M. Roberts, *Statistical Auditing* (New York: AICPA, 1978): 166.

7. Ericsson and Simon, "Verbal Reports" and "Thinking-Aloud Protocols."

CHAPTER 11

Protocol Analysis of Auditor Decision Processes and Criteria Usage

This chapter uses verbal protocol analysis to investigate both the underlying information search and decision process auditors used to complete the Olde Oak case and the criteria they used in reaching their various decisions and judgments.

Several questions derived from the experimental results discussed earlier, including the question of *comprehensiveness* of the subjects' information search behavior, led to a protocol study of the subjects' completion of the task. The use of verbal protocol analysis provides evidence of the actual decision processes used by auditors in searching for data, in evaluating alternative recommendations, and in reaching a decision. Some evidence concerning decision heuristics and the criteria considered by the auditors is also obtained.

PROTOCOL ANALYSIS OF AUDITORS' VERBALIZATIONS OF THEIR DECISION PROCESSES[1]

The evaluation of internal controls and subsequent integration of this evaluation into the audit planning decision is by any standard a highly complex task. Little is known, however, about the auditor's information search and decision processes. Most early research in this area suggested that certain judgments related to internal control evaluation could be represented by a simple linear decision rule.[2] On the surface, at least, these findings represent a paradox. How can simple linear decision rules represent a decision that seems highly complex and nonlinear? The paradox may be explained by two observations. First, the research studies cited above involved task situations that were simplified so that subjects could make repeated judgments on a number of cases within a relatively short period of time. This allowed the application of statistical models to the experimental results, but the experimental task may not have captured the complexity of the task that the practicing auditor faces. Second, the linear models in those studies were representational models and therefore were not necessarily descriptive of how individual subjects actually processed information in making their judgments.

One possible solution to this problem is to use verbal protocol analysis. In verbal protocol analysis, subjects are given a task and are asked to think aloud as they make their decisions. A model of each subject's problem-solving behavior is developed from the verbalizations (verbal protocols). Thus, verbal protocol analysis provides a basis for developing a trace of subjects' step-by-step information processing as they make a complex decision.

GENERAL RESEARCH QUESTIONS

Verbal protocol analysis might be expected to provide answers to the following types of general research questions:[3]

1. What decision models describe an individual auditor's study and evaluation of internal accounting controls and design of related audit programs?

2. What are the step-by-step processes used by auditors to make a complex internal control evaluation?

   a. What information search patterns are used?

   b. How much information is explicitly referenced?

c. How do auditors process the information and knowledge related to the evaluation of internal controls and related audit program decisions?

d. What types of analytical processes or *operators* are used, and what is their frequency?

e. What types of decision rules, heuristics, conjectures, and assumptions are being used or being made?

f. Are there some general patterns that characterize their decision behavior?

One reason that research has ignored studying questions such as these is that the methodology for data collection and data analysis is not well known. However, verbal protocol analysis has been used to study decision-making in a variety of highly complex situations, such as financial analysis, chess playing and arithmetical tasks.[4]

Tasks and Subjects

Four experienced audit seniors were the subjects. The task was the one discussed in chapter 5 and Appendix A where two of the subjects solved cases with fair and two with strong internal accounting control treatments. Compared to the experiments, the only differences were that the case materials were put into audit binders and the subjects were given a practice session on an accounting task to become familiar with the tape recording process.

Data Collection

The subjects were asked to think aloud as they performed the task, and their verbalizations were recorded on audio tape. The tape recordings were transcribed into short phrases in accordance with procedures established by Newell and Simon.[5] An example of such a transcript from Subject B is shown in figure 11.1.

Verbal Protocol Scoring Procedures

Each subject's protocol was scored by two researchers to identify the types of operations performed (termed operators), data sources referenced, and decision heuristics used by each subject. By preparing and reconciling a preliminary coding of two subjects' protocols, a list of operators being used was developed. This list, which is detailed in figure 11.2, contains operators representing subjects' task structuring, information search, analysis, and decision activities. Formal scoring (coding) rules were developed and applied to all four subjects, and differences were reconciled.

Figure 11.1
Example of Protocol Transcript From Subject B

Line Number	Verbal Protocol
906	this, the attribute sample test. It just might not be,
907	it might not be the proper use of the test itself,
908	in the fact that we are not addressing the identified strengths
909	in two out of the three tests,
910	which is cause for concern.
911	It seems to be. . .
	(Here again, you're on E-6, are you?)
912	Yes, I'm just now, I'm just going to basically review the entire program,
913	just to highlight what we've already discussed
914	and possible revisions.
915	Again, these random selections are still,
916	they just really seem to be. . .
917	We did it last year, they probably did it the year before,
918	so why not do it this year?
919	These selections should be based on the results of the prior year result,
920	of prior year test work,
921	and detailed it accordingly, either increase or decrease.

To determine the reliability of the verbal protocol scoring, a measure termed the Kappa Coefficient was used to determine the amount of nonchance agreement between the two researchers.[6] A Kappa Coefficient of 55 percent, which is statistically significant, was obtained.

Basic Results

The research results obtained from the protocol study include evidence concerning auditors' information search and decision processes. The evidence indicates a rather complex task requiring a significant amount of information search and analytical operations. The evidence may be analyzed at both a micro- and a macro- level. Micro-level analysis focuses on the specific operators used, whereas macro-level analysis attempts to capture the overall aspects of the auditor's decision process.

Figure 11.3 contains a summary of the frequency with which operators were assigned to each auditor. Figure 11.3 also includes the number of pages and lines in each verbal protocol. On average, information search encompassed 39 percent and analysis 54 percent of the assigned operators. Subjects generated and evaluated numerous alternative solutions. Task uncertainty is evident in the large number of explicit conjectures and assumptions that were stated.

The time, about two hours, required to complete the task was approximately the same for the protocol and experimental subjects discussed in previous chapters. The completion of the task generated an average of over 1,400 lines of text, most of which contain a complete sentence or thought.

The protocols were examined for overall or macro indicators of behavior, including the completeness of subjects' information search, systematic decision process patterns, and evidence of decision heuristics. The results are summarized in figure 11.4. Completeness of information search is indicated by the ratio of the number of items of information explicitly referenced through information search operations and total items of information (144) contained in the case materials. As is evident in figure 11.4, subjects A and C explicitly searched out over 85 percent of the items. This represents evidence of comprehensive information

Figure 11.2
Operators and Operator Definitions
Used in Coding of Verbal Protocols

Operator	Notation	Brief Description*

Task Structuring
1. Set goal — SG — Assigned when subject specifies a goal to be accomplished in performing the sample size decision. The SG operator usually signifies the beginning of an "episode" or "sub-episode."

Information Search
2. Information search — IS — Assigned when subject searches the case materials for specific pieces of information (directed search) or searches following some systematic pattern (usually sequential search). A piece of information is defined as all the words contained under one label (section) in the case materials.

3. Algebraic calculation — AC — Assigned when subject makes a mathematical calculation in order to obtain new information about the task.

4. Information retrieval — IR — Assigned when subject retrieves a previously stored piece of information from external memory (i.e., notes, calculations) or internal memory.

Operator	Notation	Brief Description*

Analytical
5. Assumption   AS   Assigned when subject generates an arbitrary (unspecified) fact about the case.

6. Conjecture   CJ   Assigned when subject makes an if-then or hypothetical statement.

7. Comparison   CN   Assigned when subject makes a judgment based on a comparative process (i.e., two alternatives, the current and prior year's programs.

8. Evaluation   E   Assigned when subject makes a teleological judgment about the task based on some explicit or implicit criterion.

9. Generate alternative   GA   Assigned when subject specifically states a tentative sample size alternative.

10. Generate query   GQ   Assigned when subject raises a question about the task.

Decision Process
11. Decision rule   DR   Assigned when subject specifies a method (including heuristics) of determining a sample size or parameters (i.e., stratification) directly related to the sample size decision.

Operator	Notation	Brief Description*
12. Sample size	SS	Assigned when subject finalizes
13. Temporary Sample		the sample size (SS) or specifies a
size	TSS	temporary sample size size (TSS)
		that is ultimately revised.
14. Other decisions	OD	Assigned when subject recommends that other actions be taken (i.e., "must consult with manager," or recommends an additional audit procedure).

---

* The actual definitions used were more detailed and contained examples.

Figure 11.3
Frequency of Operator Use by Protocol Subjects
and Measures of Length of Protocol

	Subject A	Subject B	Subject C	Subject D
Task Structuring Operator				
Set goal (SG)	8	20	13	4
Information Search Operators				
Information search (IS)	189	148	165	53
Algebraic calculation (AC)	23	31	6	5
Information retrieval (IR)	7	23	8	15
Analytical Process Operators				
Evaluation (E)	237	159	166	29
Generate alternative (GA)	42	42	47	9
Generate query (GQ)	49	41	1	7
Conjecture (CJ)	45	9	15	7
Assumption (AS)	0	9	5	2
Comparison (CN)	48	29	30	5
Decision Process Operators				
Decision rule (DR)	0	3	1	2
Temporary sample size decision (TSS)	3	2	4	5
Sample size decision (SS)	11	7	7	5
Other decisions (OD)	31	10	19	7
Total Identified (Coded) Operators	693	533	487	155
Length of Typed Protocol				
Number of pages	62	70	60	19
Number of lines	1,449	2,015	1,726	477

search, and also is correlated with our characterization of these subjects' decision processes.

The issue of decision process was investigated by use of episode and problem behavior graph analysis.[7] First, a number of theoretical decision models and approaches were considered. However, most of the existing theoretical models ignore information search, which is an important part of the task in this study. One possible combined information search and choice model is reproduced as figure 11.5. This model addresses the task of recommending a sample size in terms of set goal, information search, and decision operations.

According to the analysis conducted, the subjects tended to use one of two strategies:

• Systematic Search Strategy—This strategy involved a comprehensive search of available information and the information system before any attempt to make an extent decision.

• Directed Search Strategy—This strategy involved the selection of a particular audit step and then a search for information relevant to the sample size decision for that audit step alone. Once that decision was made, a similar process was employed on the next audit step. Thus, there was a particular information search for each audit step.

Subjects A and C used a *systematic search* that entailed first an in-depth review of the environmental data, the planning data, and the information system flow charts. Subject D used a *directed search* process, which began with selection of a specific audit procedure and continued with a search of the materials in terms of their relevance to that procedure. Subject B used a hybrid approach in which the search and evaluation operations were directed by a sequential consideration of all audit program steps (E-1 through E-16).

Thus, although not conclusive, this phase of the research provides some insight into the comprehensiveness of information search (up to 88 percent of available data) and the decision processes that were used. It also provides some evidence of the decision heuristics used by subjects. Figure 11.4 indicates that anchoring was evident in all four subjects and

Figure 11.4
Subjects' Information Search and Decision

	Subject A	Subject B	Subject C	Subject D
Proportion of 144 information items referenced	86.1%	47.2%	88.2%	35%
Characterization of subject's decision process	Systematic search	Systematic search directed by audit program	Systematic search	Search directed by four reviewed procedures
Evidence of decision heuristics	Possible anchoring, rule of thumb for confirmation stratification	Anchoring	Anchoring, halo effect	Anchoring

Figure 11.5
One Possible Decision Process Flowchart

Task — Recommend a sample size for audit procedure E-N

Episode I — Goal: Determine nature and objective of the audit procedure

1. Determine the account (and related transactions) being audited

2. Determine test objectives
   a. What are the implied risks?

3. Determine planned audit procedures
   a. Nature
   b. Extent
   c. Timing
   d. Prior evidence and rationale

Episode II — Goal: Determine to what extent the system may be relied on

4. Gain an understanding of the system
   a. Controls
   b. Strengths and weaknesses
   c. Possible errors

5. How was the system audited?
   a. What compliance tests were conducted?
   b. What were the test results?

6. Determine what reliance may be placed
   a. What reliance did the manager place?
   b. Accept or reassess?
   c. Reliance decision

Episode III — Goal: Reach a sample size recommendation

7. What other audit evidence is relevant?
   a. Are there substitute procedures?
   b. Does interrelated, complementary, or compensating evidence exit?

8. What are the costs and benefits of the alternatives?

9. Determine the sample size

that subject B used a rule of thumb in stratifying his confirmations (to gain greater dollar coverage). The protocols contained explicit anchoring references, such as that reproduced in protocol lines 917 and 921 in the excerpt from subject B's protocol reproduced earlier in this chapter.

PROTOCOL ANALYSIS OF CRITERIA AUDITORS UTILIZE IN THE EVALUATION OF INTERNAL ACCOUNTING CONTROLS

The evaluation of internal controls and the subsequent integration of this evaluation into the audit planning decisions is, by any standard, a highly complex task. In order to make these decisions, the auditor must collect and evaluate a considerable amount of information. Furthermore, in evaluating this information, auditors are expected to take into account *multiple criteria*. For example, the multiple criteria referenced in the professional literature relate to audit risk, control adequacy, materiality, cost, and statistical criteria such as beta risk. The auditor's decision process can be viewed as one involving evaluation of numerous pieces of information, and each evaluation may involve a complex trade-off among multiple criteria. In this section, research is reported which examines the criteria employed by the four experienced auditors who solved the Olde Oak Case while verbal protocols were being collected.

The purpose of the analysis is to explore in detail the criteria and related evaluations the auditors actually utilized the Olde Oak setting. Such an exploration should help us understand the complex, multi-criteria setting that underlies professional auditor judgment. It may also help explain the variability which was presented in Chapter 8 and which has been observed in many other audit settings.[8]

ADDITIONAL RESEARCH QUESTIONS

The research questions addressed in this section ask:

3. What criteria do auditors utilize as they evaluate systems of internal accounting controls,

4. How are these criteria used to weigh, filter, and compare the various information items (cues) available in an audit task, and

5. What differences exist between auditors in their use of and emphasis on audit criteria?

Research aimed at these types of questions is based on the premise that an improved understanding of auditors' decision processes, especially with respect to multiple criteria, will facilitate both improved professional standards as a result of improved normative models or improved descriptive models of "professional judgment".

VERBAL PROTOCOL SCORING PROCEDURES AND THE IDENTIFICATION OF UNDERLYING CRITERIA[9]

Recall that the subjects' protocols were independently scored by each researcher to identify the operators, data sources, and decision heuristics used. Non-chance agreement measured by the Kappa Coefficient[10] of 0.66 (p =.001) was obtained for the 2,036 operators that were coded. This percentage is reasonably high given that any particular verbalization may be classified the 14 operator categories (See Figure 11.2 for definitions of the 14 operators that were coded.)

Of particular interest to this section are the *evaluation operations* that subjects performed throughout their decision process. An evaluation was defined as follows:

> The E operator is assigned when the subject makes a teleological judgment about one or more aspects of the task and where that judgment is preliminary to a final decision concerning the sample sizes. *The evaluation must be made on the basis of explicit, implicit criterion.*

The protocols were reviewed with the objective of identifying and classifying the criteria used by subjects. Each time the subject made an evaluation, an evaluation operator was assigned. The protocols were then

Figure 11.6
Classification of Evaluation Criteria

Criteria Category	Description
[1] Qualities of an audit procedure	Evaluation based on the objective of an audit procedure, its nature, scope or timing or its importance and information content
[2] Audit risk or exposure	Evaluation based on the audit risk or exposure evident in a specific situation
[3] Qualities of accounting controls	Evaluation based on the adequacy and reliability of a control or system strength
[4] Materiality	Evaluation based on the importance or significance of an audit situation
[5] Cost or benefit	Evaluation based on cost and/or benefits
[6] Statistical	Evaluation based upon explicit statistical sampling criteria (i.e. representative sample, confidence, etc.)
[7] Experience	Evaluation based upon past experience (aspects which seem usual, unusual, normal, abnormal, etc.)
[8] Other	Evaluations based on ambiguous or other unclassified criteria

examined to determine the explicit or implied criterion involved in each evaluation. Based upon the existing auditing literature and on the subjects' protocols, a classification scheme was developed to categorize the criteria as described in figure 11.6. This classification scheme can be viewed as one which was adequate to describe the subjects' use of criteria. To assess the reliability of this scheme, two researchers independently applied the criteria classification on a random sample of the protocols and obtained non-chance agreement[11] of 0.67. Given the detailed level of analysis the classification scheme appears to be a reliable measure of criteria used.

RESULTS AND DISCUSSION

Figure 11.7 shows the number of evaluation operators that generated a criterion that was specific enough to be included in this analysis.

Figure 11.7
Number of Evaluation Operators Generated

Auditor	No. of Evaluation Operators Generated	Percent of Total Operators Generated
A	179	34.2%
B	109	17.3%
C	135	27.0%
D	24	16.2%

Figure 11.8 contains a detailed breakdown of the frequency and percentage frequency of criteria use. It shows, for instance, that of the 179 evaluation operations that subject A made, 55 or almost 31 percent were based on criteria pertaining to various qualities of the audit procedures. These particular evaluations made reference to audit procedure qualities such as the *nature* (that is, substantive, compliance, dual-purpose), *extent* (for example, "inadequate" sample size), timing, or relevance of the evidence generated by the audit procedure.

An example of this type of evaluation can be seen in the following lines of subject B's protocol:

543   E-9, randomly select 100 invoices
544   from numerical invoice file
545   and trace totals to the accounts receivable records
546   again, this seems to be *a compliance test*

Figure 11.8
Frequency and Percentage Frequency of Auditor Criteria Usage

Criteria	Subjects			
	A	B	C	D
Qualities of	55	28	27	6
Audit Procedures	30.7%	25.6%	20.0%	25.0%
Qualities of	29	11	33	3
Accounting Controls	16.2%	10.1%	24.4%	12.5%
Cost or benefit	24	20	8	2
	13.4%	18.3%	5.9%	8.3%
Experience	24	15	10	2
	13.4%	13.8%	7.4%	8.3%
Audit Risk or	8	8	25	3
Exposure	4.5%	7.3%	18.5%	12.5%
Statistical	3	10	6	4
	1.7%	9.2%	4.4%	16.6%
Materiality	11	6	6	3
	6.1%	5.5%	4.4%	12.5%
Other	25	11	20	1
	14.0%	10.1%	14.8%	4.2%
Total	179	109	135	24

This sequence of protocols shows subject B reading the audit procedure E-9, and making a determination of the nature of the procedure. Thus the two inputs to the evaluation are procedure E-9 and subject B's intrinsic knowledge of audit procedures. From these inputs subject B concluded that E-9 is a compliance test. The evaluation operator occurs in line 546.

Figure 11.9
Minimum Number of Categories to Account for
at Least 50 Percent of Each Auditor's Criteria Usage

Criteria	Subjects				Times Included in Top 50%
	A	B	C	D	
Qualities of Audit Procedures	30.7	25.6	20.0	25.0	4
Qualities of Accounting Controls	16.2		24.4	12.5	3
Cost or benefit		18.3			1
Experience		13.8			1
Audit Risk or Exposure			18.5	12.5	2
Statistical				16.6	1
Materiality				12.5	1
Other	14.0	___	___	___	1
Total percent	60.9	57.7	62.9	79.1	
Minimum no. of categories to account for 50% of criteria usage	3	3	3	5	

A striking feature of Figure 11.9 is the extent of multiple criteria usage in the task. While criteria such as qualities of accounting procedures and controls account for fairly large percentages of the total, all auditors made frequent use of several types of criteria. Figure 11.9 shows that in order to account for at least 50 percent of each auditor's criteria usage, all eight criteria categories must be included. This illustrates the variability in approach to information evaluation by various auditors and the importance of including information concerning the various criteria in research involving auditor behavior.

Figure 11.9 also raises the issue of similarity of criteria usage across auditors. To assess this issue, several nonparametric statistical tests were conducted on the percentage frequencies shown in Figure 11.7. The results of Chi-Square tests over all auditors and for all pairs of auditors are shown in figure 11.10. The overall Chi-Square of 61.01 (p<.001) indicates little similarity in criteria usage across all auditors. However, the pairwise ChiSquares indicates some similarity in criteria usage by auditors A and B.[12] However, the Chi-Square tests generally reveal little similarity in criteria usage.

Figure 11.10
Chi-Square Values on Relative Criteria Usage
for all Pairs of Auditors
(Significance Levels in Parentheses)

		Subject		
		A	B	C
	B	8.12		
		(0.30)		
Subject	C	17.61	23.74	
		(0.02)	(0.01)	
	D	28.86	15.30	24.47
		(0.001)	(0.05)	(0.001)

To further assess the similarity issue, more aggregate ranking tests were performed.[13] First, Kendall's Coefficient of Concordance, W, of .463 was significant at the 0.1 level.[14] This reveals that, over all auditors, the rankings of criteria usage were somewhat similar. Auditors A and B, and A and C also show rank correlation significant at the 0.05 level, while negative or small correlations were obtained between the other pairs of auditors. The significance of W seems to be primarily due to the correlations of B and C with A.

In reviewing the data it is not possible to say that one approach characterized all the auditors' criteria usage. Based on both Chi-Square and rank order correlation, it appears that auditors A and B had a similar pattern of criteria usage, but there is little similarity among the other auditors. Further, a large proportion of the auditors' evaluations involved criteria related to qualities of audit procedures and controls.

The criteria data also indicate some possible differences in what could be called "decision styles" among auditors. For instance, subject C seemed to concentrate heavily on evaluations of the audit risks and exposures evident in the accounting system and the various qualities of the accounting controls which may relate directly to such risks and exposures. Subject C's profile is consistent with an "risk model analysis" decision style in that it contains higher relative risk and control-quality criteria than any of the other subjects. In contrast, subject A explicated evaluations which emphasize relatively few explicit references to audit risk or materiality. Such a decision style might be labeled "information content focused" in the sense that subject A was most concerned with the quality of the evidence produced by the various audit procedures.

GENERAL OBSERVATIONS AND IMPLICATIONS

Some additional general observations may be made with respect to the primary research questions addressed in this section. Our first concern was with the number and kinds of criteria auditors actually utilize in audit decision making. In this study, eight categories of criteria were identified in the subjects' verbal protocols. Further, the data showed that the actual audit decision processes were quite complex, encompassing the use of all eight classes of criteria that were identified.

Problems that require the use of multiple criteria involve complex, often subjective, trading-off and weighing of criteria. For many such problems no optimal trade-off scheme can be derived, particularly when two or more individuals are involved. This implies that the derivation of an optimal, normative decision rule for such auditor decisions may be impossible. Thus the judgmental, hierarchical, group decision process observed in actual audits may be a viable solution and perhaps be the only feasible solution to this type of problem solving. This raises very difficult issues for audit standard setters who seek to specify norms for internal control evaluation and other audit activities.

Another general observation involves the assessment of the similarity in subjects' relative use of criteria in their evaluation process. The significant coefficient of concordance and positive rank-order correlation indicates some similarity in criteria usage. This contrasts somewhat with the significant amount of unexplained variability that were observed in the auditors' decisions in chapter 8.

Lastly, the protocols and content analysis jointly have led to a set of criteria that empirically form the basis of auditors' study and evaluation of internal accounting control systems. Unless some of these criteria can be shown to be irrelevant, they should be explicitly considered by researchers and practitioners alike.

LIMITATIONS

Like most other research methods, protocol analysis exhibits both strengths and limitations. Limitations include the possibility that the verbalization and taping might have had an obtrusive effect on the subjects.[15] Also, costs of transcribing, coding, and analyzing the protocols tend to prohibit large sample sizes. Finally, there is now no standard set of operators for a typical audit task, nor has any standard method of characterizing decision processes been developed.

SUMMARY

This chapter has presented the results of a protocol study of the subjects' information search and sample size choice processes. The protocol study indicated up to 88 percent comprehensiveness in subjects' information search of the provided audit materials. However, although the subjects attended to a large percentage of the audit materials, a very small proportion of the possible relevant factors ended up in their rationale memos (see the previous chapter).

The protocol analysis identified three general categories of operators that subjects used: (1) information search, (2) analytical, and (3) choice.

On average, 93 percent of the subjects' decision activities were devoted to information search and analytical operations.

The protocol analysis also helped identify two general strategies that auditors seemed to use in this task—a search directed primarily by each audit procedure and a systematic search focused initially on gaining an understanding of the accounting system. Such differences in search strategy could have important implications for auditor decision-making. Lastly, a detailed study of the criteria that auditors utilize in this task was presented.

NOTES

1. This chapter integrates many of the key results from Stanley R. Biggs and Theodore J. Mock, "An Investigation of Auditor Decision Processes in the Evaluation of Internal Controls and Audit Scope Decisions," *Journal of Accounting Research* (Spring 1983), and Stanley R. Biggs and Theodore J. Mock, "Criteria Auditors Utilize in the Evaluation of Internal Accounting Control," *Pacific Accounting Review* (January 1989): 59-75.

2. Robert H. Ashton, "An Experimental Study of Internal Control Judgments," *Journal of Accounting Research* 12 (Spring 1974): 143-57; and Edward J. Joyce, "Expert Judgment in Audit Program Planning," *Studies on Human Information Processing in Accounting,* Supplement to *Journal of Accounting Research* 14 (1976): 29-60.

3. Criteria-related research questions are discussed later in this chapter.

4. Allen Newell and Herbert Simon, *Human Problem Solving* (Englewood Cliffs, N.J.: Prentice-Hall, 1972) and K. Anders Ericsson and Herbert A. Simon, *Protocol Analysis*, The MIT Press, (2nd. Ed.) 1993.

5. *Ibid,* p. 166.

6. Jacob Cohen, "A Coefficient of Agreement for Nominal Scales," *Educational and Psychological Measurement* 20 (Spring 1960): 37-46.

7. See Newell and Simon, *Human Problem Solving,* and Stanley F. Biggs, "An Investigation of the Decision Processes Underlying the Assessment of Corporate Earning Power" (Ph.D. diss. University of Minnesota, 1978).

8. See, among others, Robert H. Ashton, "Cue Utilization and Expert Judgments: A Comparison of Independent Auditors with other Judges," *Journal of Applied Psychology* 59 (August 1974): 437-444; Robert H. Ashton and Paul R. Brown, "Descriptive Modeling of Auditors' Internal Control Judgments: Replication and Extension," *Journal of Accounting Research* 18 (Spring 1980): 269-278; Edward .J. Joyce, "Expert Judgment in Audit Program Planning," Supplement to *Journal of Accounting Research* 14 (1976): 29-60; R.E. Hamilton and W.F. Wright, "Internal Control Judgments and Effects of Experience: Replications and Extensions," *Journal of Accounting Research* 20 (Spring 1982): 756-765. B.R. Gaumnitz, T.R. Nunamaker, J.J. Surdick, and M.F. Thomas, "Auditor Consensus in Internal Control Evaluation and Audit Program Planning," *Journal of Accounting Research* 20 (Autumn 1982): 745-755.

9. Coding details are described in Biggs and Mock, "An Investigation of Auditor Decision Processes in the Evaluation of Internal Controls and Audit Scope Decisions." Protocol coding approaches and issues in accounting and auditing research are discussed in G. Klersey and Theodore J. Mock, "Verbal Protocol Research in Auditing," *Accounting, Organizations, and Society* 14 (1989): 131-151.

10. Cohen, "A Coefficient of Agreement for Nominal Scales."

11. *Ibid.*

12. Although it is questionable whether or not the data meets assumptions required for assessing their significance, product moment correlations were calculated. These results reinforce the results of the nonparametric tests revealing only auditors A and B as having a large correlation (0.849, p<.05).

13. See Biggs and Mock, "Criteria Auditors Utilize in the Evaluation of Internal Accounting Control."

14. S. Siegel, *Nonparametric Statistics for the Behavioral Sciences*, (New York: McGraw-Hill, 1956)

15. However, research to date indicates little likelihood of obtrusive effects in properly designed protocol studies. See K.A. Ericsson and H. A. Simons, *Protocol Analysis: Verbal Reports as Data*, (Cambridge, MA: The MIT Press, 1984) and Klersey and Mock, "Verbal Protocol Research in Accounting,": 133-52.

CHAPTER 12

Summary, Implications and Implementation

Although the subject of internal accounting controls continues to receive significant attention within the audit profession, in the 1970s the topic was particularly prominent. Important events during this period included the promulgation of ASR 173 and the passage of the Foreign Corrupt Practices Act. Unfortunately, when practitioners looked for existing research and to academic researchers for knowledge that might help with issues such as internal accounting control evaluation, it was readily apparent that little was available.

In 1977, the "Big 8" audit firm of Peat Marwick Mitchell & Co. (now KPMG Peat Marwick) began two parallel research efforts aimed at enhancing audit research. The first effort was the Research Opportunities in Auditing (ROA) program. The chief element of this program was a research grant competition in which approximately ten academic research projects were selected and funded annually. A less well known effort was Peat Marwick's in-house research program where academics were selected to spend one or more years within the firm conducting research on an agenda of research issues generated by Peat Marwick.

The first of these in-house research efforts resulted in the series of studies that have been detailed in the prior chapters of this Anthology. This final chapter first presents an overview of the most important research findings. In addition, it summarizes the implementation phase of the research that ultimately led to Peat Marwick's SEADOC—System Evaluation Approach, Documentation of Controls.

Although the implications of research findings and future research paths are, to a great extent, the bottom line of a research project, the reader should be aware of the difficulties in drawing generalizations and implications from research. Most research is based on a number of critical assumptions and is constrained by a number of limitations. This study is no exception, although it does exhibit advantages over many previous audit research studies—the use of multiple experiments, adequate sample size, actual auditor subjects, and highly motivated subjects. Many of the possible limitations of this study have been discussed in preceding chapters and need not be repeated.

The research findings of this study cover a wide range of factors and circumstances. These multiple results make implications even more difficult to draw than would be the case in a more typical one- or two-factor research study. The major research implications and related future research questions may be discussed in terms of six types of findings:

(1) variability among auditors in their various recommendations, judgments, and interpretations,
(2) documentation of auditor rationale,
(3) the effect of auditor guidance,
(4) the effect of the audit review process,
(5) behavioral factors, and
(6) the impact of task complexity.

VARIABILITY

The analysis of auditors' decision processes concerning internal accounting controls contained in chapters 2, 3, 4, and 6 identified many relevant variables that might impact audit judgments concerning internal control evaluations. These included combined audit risk factors, relevant internal controls, the internal control environment, and trade-offs in nature, timing, and extent of alternative packages of audit procedures. It is not surprising, then, that the actual sample size decisions and rationale documentation exhibited a great deal of variability among auditors.

Variability was observed in terms of the factors that are inputs into auditors' sample size recommendations, including their interpretation of the nature (substantive, compliance, dual purpose) of the audit procedures, their judgments about appropriate alpha risk, beta risk, and materiality, the relevance of various internal control strengths and the amount of reliance that they were willing to place on the compliance-tested strengths. Also their information search and decision strategies varied considerably as evidenced in a protocol study.

Perhaps even more surprising was the rather small percentage of variability initially explained by the various statistical models utilized in chapter 8 and given the number of possible explanatory factors included in the analysis. However, using statistical methods based on the general linear model, chapter 9 presented improved descriptive models of auditor judgment by utilizing multivariate analysis. Chapter 9 also more thoroughly considered the issue of adequacy of auditor judgment documentation. This issue was not previously examined in the original Mock and Turner monograph.[1]

In general, the multivariate models were found to be quite complex with several models containing significant interaction terms. These findings imply that auditor judgments may have been *nonlinear* or *nonconfigural*. More recent research by Brown and Solomon and by Trotman has also resulted in similar findings.[2]

In comparison to the variance explained by the experimental treatments alone, models based upon data developed from both concurrent and retrospective documentation were derived in chapter 9 which exhibited greater explained variance (adjusted R^2s). In addition to explaining more variance, these models were found to be robust both with respect to predictive validity and various residual analyses.

Given the concurrent documentation experiment, the derived judgment models for all audit procedures may be interpreted as anchoring and adjustment heuristics based on either a minimum or maximum sample size judgment. Although some evidence of individual specific (idiosyncratic) behavior was obtained, general (nomothetic) models were found to describe a substantial amount of the observed variance in auditor judgments. However, much variance in audit judgment remained unexplained even given the more complex statistical modeling of chapter 9 and given the extensive set of explanatory variable considered.

The major implication of (unexplained) variability in sample size recommendations concerns the possible risk of unwarranted reliance on small sample sizes and the risk of excessive audit cost for large samples.

Such risks may be directly related to decision variability only if other audit planning factors remain constant. The magnitude of such risks can only be measured if future research studies can quantitatively relate the quality of internal controls to the many other variables in the audit, including ultimate audit risk, probability of material error or irregularity, and audit cost. Such a normative solution to the experimental case study was not obtained.

If such risks are deemed significant in practice, it might be desirable to reduce sample size variability possibly through the review process, through a narrowing of decision alternatives by specifying standards or ranges, and perhaps through elimination of certain judgments by automating them. Such approaches were considered in the implementation phase of this study to be discussed later.

The second aspect of observed variability concerns the lack of explained variance in terms of the statistically evaluated variables. For the sample size decisions, this implies that many decision variables and decision approaches may have been used by the various auditors. For the observed variability in rationale documentation, this could lead to difficulties in communication and thus in review. Issues concerning rationale documentation are discussed in the following section.

In general, lack of explained variability shows that too little is known about the complex decision processes underlying internal accounting control evaluation and rationale documentation.

RATIONALE DOCUMENTATION

As noted in chapters 8 and 9, rationale documentation was not comprehensive when compared to a twelve-cue dictionary of items that would help justify an audit sample size recommendation. Comprehensiveness was increased by the guidance provided in three of the experiments, but memo content varied significantly among auditors and audit teams. In most cases, rationale documentation followed the auditors review of the audit materials and thus was prepared after each decision (retrospectively) rather than concurrently with the decision process. Given the task's complexity and the retrospective nature of the documentation, lack of comprehensiveness was not surprising.

Although both the open-ended (retrospective) and structured (concurrent) methods were found lacking in comprehensiveness in chapter 8, in chapter 9 careful study and coding of the documentation produced by both methods led to models with statistically higher descriptive and predictive characteristics. In the cases of the transaction cycle audit procedures (E-5, E-6 and E-9), the structured, concurrent method produced a greater amount of explained variance. In the case of a test of account balances, the open-ended, retrospective method led to higher explained variance.

The results imply that formal decision documentation methods may need to be improved and that alternative means of documentation need to be developed and tested. Alternatives include concurrent documentation through structured planning forms or through automation of internal control evaluation. Such automation would be similar to what is frequently done in computer-assisted statistical sampling, in which key decisions are input to the system and may be permanently stored in memory.

Of course, the desirability of such possible improvement is basically a cost/benefit question and a question that was addressed in the implementation phase of the research discussed later. However, the experimental research alone does indicate that open-ended, narrative rationale memos are unsatisfactory in many respects.

GUIDANCE

The auditing profession invests significant resources in formal training and audit program guidance. Thus, research on the impact of the effect and effectiveness of various types of guidance should be welcomed. In this research study, several types of guidance experiments were designed and implemented following the first two experiments. Guidance tested included both the structured-guidance experiment and the guidance provided in the statistical and manager-review experiments. Although the guidance provided had no statistically significant effect on sample size decision variability, the guidance did increase the comprehensiveness of rationale documentation. Also, the behavioral *halo effect* observed in the two early experiments was not significant in the latter experiments in which internal control evaluation guidance was provided.

Although these results imply that such guidance may be useful, the cost/benefit aspects are unclear. As noted, other experimental results, such as unexplained variability, may indicate that improved guidance or decision aids need to be developed and tested.

REVIEW PROCESS, MULTI-PERSON EFFECTS AND BEHAVIORAL FACTORS

In addition to the results and implications already summarized, some limited results were obtained with respect to the audit review process and several investigated behavioral factors. For example, the manager-review experiment involved thirty audit senior-audit manager teams in which a manager reviewed the senior's recommendations and rationale memos. Then both auditors met and jointly reached a decision. Their joint results did not differ significantly from the individual auditor decisions in terms of sample size, sample size variability, or content of their rational memos. Little research has been conducted within an auditing context on group or joint decisions; thus, it is difficult to speculate about the factors that may have led to these findings. The most obvious hypothesis relates to the relatively limited comprehensiveness of the narrative rationale memos coupled with the task's complexity. These two factors may have mitigated any potential review effect. Perhaps research into content analysis of rationale documentation and other review techniques is needed. Perhaps standardized documentation (e.g. KPMG's SEADOC approach) and approval forms are indicated.

The results obtained with respect to behavioral factors are limited since they encompassed secondary research objectives. Yet some evidence was obtained that indicated possible *halo effects*, where the auditor reduced a sample size decision on the basis of general improvement in internal accounting controls rather than specific, directly related controls. Subjects also seemed to *anchor* on previously planned sample sizes.

Both content analysis of rationale memos and a protocol study of selected auditors' information search and decision processes indicated anchoring, use of rules of thumb (heuristics), and substantial differences in search and choice models. These results support the increasing amount of behavioral auditing research that is now occurring. Educational programs that may increase an auditor's awareness of behavioral factors are also indicated.

The experimental findings with respect to halo effect and possible anchoring may have implications for the preparation of audit programs. If halo effect is shown to impair appropriate weighting of specific control improvements, auditors could be instructed to make sharper distinctions between improvements in general and specific internal controls. If anchoring is shown to be a barrier to determining appropriate sample size, it may be advisable to design the planning process so that anchors are not available. The results obtained in the guidance versions of the experiments also indicate that structured documentation forms and formal review may counteract such factors and behavioral tendencies.

TASK COMPLEXITY

Perhaps the most pervasive finding that arose both from the experimental and review phases of this study concerns the significant complexity involved in internal accounting control evaluation. This conclusion is valid even from the limited perspective of an external auditor reviewing controls purely as an input into audit program design. Internal control reviews with more general objectives (such as that indicated in the COSO study) would seem to exhibit even greater complexity. Task complexity was evident in a number of findings:

- A large number of information inputs are required (see figures 5.3, 6.1, 6.2, and 9.11 and Appendix A).

- A significant number of interrelated auditor judgments are required (see figure 5.2).

- Lack of professional consensus, and thus ambiguity, exists with respect to many of the input cues. For example, judgments varied considerably in terms of auditors' interpretation of the nature of audit evidence, relationships among test objectives, compliance test results, and related substantive tests.

- Lack of statistical or judgmental decision norms exists. Unambiguous, normative decision rules have yet to be derived concerning many factors, including appropriate conditions for reliance and trade-offs among audit risk and cost factors.

- Numerous approaches and techniques exist to identify, document, and evaluate internal accounting controls (see chapter 4).

- No method has yet been implemented for cost/benefit analysis although a notion of net benefit is contained in the second and third standards of audit field work.

These items imply that further research is needed. It should be noted, though, that research on complex decision situations, ill-structured decisions, and group decision-making is still somewhat primitive. Thus, short-term breakthroughs may be unlikely. Task complexity may also indicate that the auditing profession may require an experimental and developmental period before resolving the issues related to the continued interest in internal control systems.

**IMPLEMENTATION OF RESEARCH FINDINGS:
THE SEADOC SAGA[3]**

As indicated earlier, the experiments discussed in this Anthology were the first of a series of in-house research efforts conducted as part of KPMG's ROA program. Specifically, the basic experimental and protocol research ultimately led to SEADOC—Peat Marwick's System Evaluation Approach, Documentation of Controls. A discussion of the important implementation efforts that led to the ultimate use of SEADOC within KPMG follow.

SEADOC, a system for documenting internal accounting controls and a decision aid for evaluating accounting control systems, was in essence an extension of SEA (System Evaluation Approach), Peat Marwick's method of documenting internal controls in the 1970s. SEA relied heavily on flowcharting of accounting systems. However little information concerning controls, especially as to how control strengths or weaknesses might relate to an appropriate audit program, was contained in SEA. The research and implementation process that led to SEADOC involved both a basic research phase and a field test phase.

The Basic Research Phase

The basic research began in 1977 with the research plan described earlier in chapters 5 and 6 designed to address the following questions:

- To what extent and in what manner do experienced auditors respond to different evidence of the effectiveness of internal controls?

- What factors do they consider in making and in justifying their audit procedure planning judgments?

- Are their decisions influenced by different types of audit decision aids, guidance, and approaches?

- Are their decisions influenced by heuristics, training, experience, or other behavioral differences?

A three-phased, multi-method research approach was employed to address these issues and others that arose during the course of the research. Phases I and II consisted of the series of five related field experiments discussed earlier where experienced auditors completed the Olde Oak case study. The primary decision task for the auditors was to provide sample size recommendations and a related rationale memo for each of four planned audit procedures. Phase III was the protocol study discussed in chapters 10 and 11 which utilized process-tracing techniques, again using experienced auditors solving the same realistic audit case.

As noted, the general results of the basic research phases showed that the study and evaluation of internal controls is much more complex than was previously believed. Most importantly from a practice perspective, the results showed that for a sample of 200 auditors with similar amounts of training and experience:

- Significant decision variability and lack of consensus in recommendations among the auditors. A significant amount of the variability was not explainable in terms of the manipulated experimental variables or in terms of certain measured independent variables such as auditor experience, auditor training or certain psychological factors (anchoring, halo-effects, cognitive-width);

- Significant variability between auditors in their interpretations of the nature and relevance of the audit procedures, of the documented internal accounting controls, and of other audit factors;

- Significant variability in auditors' decision processes in terms of information search, alternatives considered, criteria applied, and heuristics utilized;

- Lack of comprehensiveness and clarity in the auditors' documentation of the rationale for their recommendations; and

- Evidence of questionable judgments and decision errors.

Such circumstances either may increase the possibility of unwarranted reliance on controls, thereby increasing the risk of audit failure, or may result in excessive audit costs through over-auditing. But they also provide empirical evidence and insights into means of improving the study and evaluation of systems of internal accounting controls—in short, the basis for the design and implementation phases of the research.

Over a period of approximately two years, the knowledge gained from the basic research phase plus additional research led to the design of SEADOC, a new approach which differed significantly from earlier approaches used at Peat Marwick to study internal accounting control within an audit. These differences are discussed in detail in Mock and Willingham.[4]

The Field Tests

The field tests were undertaken to satisfy the following objectives:

- Obtain additional data on the overall efficiency and effectiveness of SEADOC;

- Gain assurance as to the applicability of SEADOC to different types of entities and to entities operating in different regions including overseas locations;

- Gain assurance as to the applicability of SEADOC to computerized systems;

- Debug SEADOC documentation, procedures, and techniques;

- Determine the most effective way to bridge SEADOC results to other audit procedures; and

- Gather information on the type of training needed to fully implement SEADOC.

The Field Test Population

Twenty-two engagement teams participated in the field tests. The characteristics of this population are summarized below.

- The 22 engagement teams were from sixteen different offices, including Paris, The Hague, Frankfurt, and London;

- In addition to several manufacturing companies, the clients included representatives of the savings and loan, banking, education, printing, retailing, freight forwarding, and oil and gas industries;
- The clients ranged in size from $700,000 to $864,000,000 in total assets and from $300,000 to $1.4 billion in total revenues;

- Total audit hours of the field test engagements ranged from 175 to 4,000. Total audit hours of seven of the 22 engagements were 500 or fewer, whereas eight of the 22 were 1,000 or more;

- The areas chosen by the engagement teams for field test work covered all of the traditional accounting "cycles"— revenue, purchases, inventory, and payroll. Three engagement teams applied SEADOC to an entire company.

The fields tests led to the expectation that a 17 percent reduction in audit hours would be realized for new clients. Perhaps more importantly, the new documentation proved to be more effective in identifying strengths and weaknesses, and it produced more consistent documentation from client to client and from auditor to auditor. It is always difficult to realize both increased efficiency and increased effectiveness with any innovation, but the Peat Marwick experience with SEADOC has shown it is possible.

However, SEADOC was not the sole outcome of the experimental and protocol research presented in earlier chapters. Two sampling decision-aids were developed, both based on mathematical models. One was designed to determine compliance-tests sample sizes after controls are documented and analyzed. The other was designed to determine substantive-test sample sizes after controls have been tested. These decision aids together with SEADOC were a response to the original research findings on variability in auditors' sample-size decisions.

An additional result of the in-house research that led to SEADOC was an attempt to improve the various Peat Marwick audit training courses. Part of this process included consulting a number of academics concerning materials and content of their courses. This led to the inclusion of materials related to the role of heuristics and biases in audit judgment, the use of structured decision approaches, etc.

Evolution of SEADOC at KPMG Peat Marwick

Although SEADOC provided Peat Marwick with a measurable competitive advantage during the early- and mid-1980s, both external and internal influences led to a gradual phase out of the SEADOC approach. One external influence was a change in technology used by clients. During the period when SEADOC was designed and first implemented, most accounting systems in large companies were mainframe-oriented. While the mainframe computer was used to process data, typical accounting systems included extensive manual procedures, and, accordingly, were appropriate for documenting by the SEADOC approach. Beginning in the late 1980s, however, distributed computer systems emerged along with more on-line and real-time processing. Even though the basic concepts of SEADOC were applicable to such systems, other forms of documentation specifically tailored to EDP were found to be more efficient.

Another external influence was the response to SEADOC by competing audit firms. Although Peat Marwick may have enjoyed a competitive advantage for a period of time, all major audit firms were also attempting to implement their own more efficient control evaluation techniques. For example, Grant Thornton developed and introduced INFOCUS, an alternate approach to accounting control identification and documentation. As a result, Peat Marwick modified its documentation procedures to include more extensive use of memoranda to document the understanding of control systems and greatly reduced the amount of SEADOC flowcharting.

The primary internal influence was a major change in overall audit philosophy. Seeking an audit approach that would be both more effective and more efficient, in the mid-1990s KPMG Peat Marwick converted from the Systems Evaluation Approach to the Business Management Process (BMP) approach.[5] KPMG Peat Marwick describes BMP as a "holistic" approach which focuses on understanding the client's business and processes to develop an audit opinion rather than on performing extensive tests of controls, transactions, and balances. Once BMP was implemented, SEADOC no longer was applicable as a viable audit approach for the firm.

Of course, research questions similar to those addressed in this Anthology still need to be addressed for current audit and assurance approaches. It is unlikely that many of the issues this Anthology has discussed—decision task complexity, variability in auditor judgment and judgment documentation, use of decision heuristics, etc.—will be mitigated by or will be less of an issue for the complex systems currently being audited. Such research issues surely will be important for the broader types of judgments that will be rendered as auditors move into the provision of assurance services.

NOTES

1. Theodore J. Mock and Jerry L. Turner, AICPA Audit Research Monograph No. 3, *Internal Accounting Control and Auditor Judgment* (New York: American Institute of Certified Public Accountants, 1981).

2. See K. E. Trotman. 1985. "The review process and accuracy of auditor judgements". *Journal of Accounting Research*: 740-752 and C. E. Brown and I. Solomon. 1990. "Auditor configural information processing in control risk assessment". *Auditing: A Journal of Practice & Theory*: 17-38.

3. A more detailed historical development of SEADOC is contained in Theodore J. Mock and John J. Willingham, "An Improved Method of Documenting and Evaluating a System of Internal Accounting Control", *Auditing: A Journal of Practice & Theory* (Spring, 1983): 91-99.

4. T. J. Mock and J. J. Willingham, "An Improved Method of Documenting and Evaluating a System of Internal Controls," *Auditing: A Journal of Practice & Theory* 2(2)(1983): 91-99.

5. Timothy Bell, Frank Marrs, Ira Solomon, and Howard Thomas, *Auditing Organizations Through a Strategic-Systems Lens: The KPMG Business Management Process* (New Jersey: KPMG Peat Marwick LLP, 1997).

Appendix A

Appendix A

Olde Oak Case Materials

(For "no guidance," "fair controls" version of the case)
(Abbreviated audit program)

Biographical Data

Name _____

Office _____

Classification _____

No. of years audit experience _____

	Yes	No	If Yes, for How Long?
SAS?	_____	_____	_____
CAS?	_____	_____	_____

---

* Statistical audit specialist
** Computer audit specialist

OLDE OAK FRAMING SUPPLIES INC.
Case Study Instructions

This case has been prepared to represent a realistic audit situation concerned with the auditor's specification of the nature, extent, and timing of audit procedures. The case focuses entirely on a portion of Olde Oak's revenue cycle. You are asked to assume the role of the new in-charge accountant for Olde Oak who has been a client for several years. In the attached materials, you will find a description of your role, the client, the audit programs for this year, bridging workpapers and other materials prepared during an audit.

Task

The major task you are asked to do is to prepare recommendations concerning the nature, extent and timing of substantive procedures.

You have been budgeted two hours to complete this task. We would recommend approximately the following time allocation.

1. Review the case materials 30 minutes

   Note: You should not critically evaluate the flowcharts, bridging workpapers, and other system documentation, but merely should familiarize yourself with the client's system. You are expected to evaluate only this year's *audit program* in regard to the nature, extent, and timing of procedures.

2. Analysis and decision about the nature, extent, 30 minutes
   and timing of substantive procedures.

3. Preparation of a rationale memo for the
   engagement manager that included your 30 minutes
   specific recommendations and documents your
   reasoning and analysis.

4. Completion of questionnaires (to be completed after step 3 is done.) 30 minutes

John Thomas, last year's senior-in-charge, left our auditing firm to head the internal audit department of one of our bank audit clients. Unfortunately, John left during this year's interim at Olde Oak Framing Supplies. You have been assigned as the new senior-in-charge and must complete interim and final audit work. After reviewing last year's and this year's workpapers and discussing the audit with the manager, Wally Barnes, you have made the following notes:

1. The program for last year and the one designed for this year are substantially the same as to nature, extent, and timing of procedures, except for step E-6 which has been modified to compliance test a new strength.

2. There were no adjusting journal entries required for any account in the revenue cycle at 12/31/76.

3. General controls appear to be good and the possibility of management override is not significant.

4. The audit manager, Wally Barnes, believes that the flowcharts are an accurate representation of the clients system and that strengths and weaknesses are properly identified on the flowcharts and the bridging workpapers. He has instructed you to evaluate the planned nature, extent and timing of the *uncompleted* interim audit steps. Specifically, he has asked you to review steps E-5, E-6, E-9, and E-10 to determine if the originally planned extent to sampling is still reasonable or appropriate in light of known changes in the system, the results of procedures already completed and his decision as to degree of reliance. Wally has asked for *specific* sizes and wants you to document your rationale in selecting these sample sizes.

5. After discussion with the assigned computer specialist, it has been decided that computer assisted auditing techniques will be used only to prepare confirmations, foot the accounts receivable file and prepare an aging of accounts receivable. *Statistical sampling will not be used for selection of sample sizes.*

6. Results of last year's compliance tests:

   a. The test for numerical sequence (E-3a, b) revealed that the clerks were not issuing invoices sequentially, they simply picked up a handy box in the supply room without regard to the numbers contained therein.

   b. The review of the packing slips (E-3c) revealed numerous sequence errors. These appeared to be a result of both the problem mentioned in (a), above, and a general laxity on the part of the dispatcher.

   c. Step E-8 revealed that the manager was performing only a *limited* review and spot-check of the monthly statements, invoices, and aged trial balance.

d. The clerk assigned the responsibility of reviewing the customer suspense file monthly was not following up on unmatched invoices (Step E-7).

e. Because of the pervasive exceptions encountered during the compliance tests, the audit team placed *no* reliance on the system of internal controls for purposes of designing substantive tests.

7. Results of last year's substantive tests:

a. The test for the reliability of the pricing and extension function indicated that there were numerous errors made when the regular clerk was ill or on vacation or when other clerks were used during high volume days. These instances occurred frequently enough to warrant a management letter comment suggesting that pricing and extensions be checked by a second clerk. They were not of such magnitude, however, as to require an adjusting journal entry as of December 31, 1976. An adjustment reflecting pricing errors noted was waived because of materiality.

b. Confirmation results are shown on an accompanying page.

8. Results of this year's compliance tests:

a. As a result of a management letter comment, the clerks have issuing invoices on a strict numerical sequence. The audit test revealed no exceptions to this control strength.

b. The review of the packing slips (E-3c) revealed only a moderate number of exceptions. These exceptions appear to be primarily due to laxity on the part the dispatcher.

c. Step E-8 revealed that the manager was still performing only a *limited* review and spot-check of the monthly statements, invoices, and aged trial balance.

    d. The clerk assigned the responsibility of reviewing the customer suspense file monthly was still not following up on unmatched invoices (Step E-7).

    e. The compliance test for clerk's initials indicating check of pricing, extensions and footings (Step E-6, a) failed on the 33rd item tested.

    f. Because the results of the compliance tests were generally better than last year, Wally Barnes has decided that we should be able to place *some* reliance on internal controls for purposes of designing this year's substantive tests.

9. Notes on this year's program:

Olde Oak installed the new internal control suggested in a previous management letter comment effective February 1, 1977, (see bridging workpapers) of having an independent check of the pricing, extension, and footing of invoices. Based on inquiry and prior years' data, it does not appear that invoices issued in January are of a different make-up than invoices issued at other times of the year. We will, therefore, test the control for an eleven-month period and extend the results to the full year. (Step E-6)

DETAILS OF ACCOUNTS RECEIVABLE
AS OF 10/31/77

Range	Number	Amount
$ 0- 500	1020	$ 250,250
500-1000	680	522,700
1000-1500	340	425,622
1500-2000	150	262,509
2000-2500	76	168,651
2500 & above	49	149,100
Total	2315	$ 1,778,832

Included in the above amounts were 45 accounts amounting to $17,652 which were past due sixty days or more.

At this point you should review the uncompleted portion of the interim program and do the following:

1. Review the sampling plans and develop specific recommendations to leave as is or change nature, extent, or timing.

2. Document your recommendations in a rationale memo, using the attached form. Please do *not* prepare a memo such as you would put in the workpapers but, instead, try to explain your true thought processes. For example, you may have considered the time budget, the manager's likes and dislikes, or other criteria or made assumptions that you would not normally document in actual workpapers. Items such as these should be in this rationale memo along with the more traditional decision factors.

Olde Oak Framing Supplies
Rationale Memo

Documentation of reasons and analysis
to be submitted to audit manager

For audit steps E-5, E-6, E-9 and E-10, indicate the rationale for all changes in the extent of recommended audit procedures. here you have indicated no change, also indicate why. Be as specific as possible about the factors that influenced your recommended sample sizes.

OLDE OAK FRAMING SUPPLIES
PLANNING MEMO
12/31/77

The Economy
Real economic growth slowed down this summer, increasing uncertainty about the durability of the current business expansion, but it is now widely believed that what lies ahead is a more modest rate of growth, rather than a recessionary trend. Preliminary government estimates of the increase in real GNP for the third quarter are in the 3 to 5% range, which contrasts to the 7.7% and 6.2% recorded for the first two quarters. At a recent meeting of

economists and business leaders sponsored by the Conference Board, an economic research organization, the consensus was that economic growth for 1978 would not exceed 4.5%. Industrial output was down .5% in August, the first decline in seven months. However, the Commerce Department's index of "leading indicators," which declined in May and June and rose only .2% in July, rose .8% in August. Inflation moderated during the summer as consumer prices rose only .4% in July and .3% in August, but government spokesmen still consider the "underlying" rate to be 6%.

The Industry

The picture frame and frame supply industry is reasonably stable, with fluctuations generally tied to economic growth or decline. The industry consists of approximately twenty large manufacturers of framing stock in the U.S. who supply a large number of wholesale outlets. The wholesale outlets, in turn, supply many small picture framing retail businesses. Product lines are stable with only a few new frame designs added each year. Accordingly, inventory levels tend to remain at a relatively constant level. Also, the retail outlets tend to purchase from the same wholesaler on a repeat basis. Competition among wholesalers is usually in the form of quantity discounts or special prices on discontinued lines.

Nature of Business

Olde Oak Framing Supplies, organized in 1938 under the laws of California, is a large wholesaler located in Los Angeles. The product line consists of finished and unfinished picture frame stock, assembled picture frames, matting, cut glass and miscellaneous related supplies. Orders are primarily received by mail with the purchaser making the selection from a catalog. Telephone orders are also received but not to the extent of mail orders.- Olde Oak Framing Supplies is the largest wholesaler on the west coast and supplies retailers as far east as St. Louis and New Orleans. All facilities are in one location in Los Angeles. Profits for the company have been stable for the last five years and are slightly above industry average.

The results of last year's confirmation work were as follows (as of 10/31/76):

Type	Total Number	Number Mailed	% Mailed	Number Received	% Received	Total Dollars	Dollars Mailed	% Mailed	Dollars Received	% Received
Past dues (P)	40	40	100.0%	20	50.0%	$ 20,400	$ 20.400	100.0%	$ 12,852	63.0%
Over $2,500 (P)	41	41	100.0	35	85.4	124,757	124,757	100.0	99,806	80.0
Under $2,500 (P)	2,051	345	16.8	265	76.8	1,544,733	248,702	16.1	196,475	79.0
Total	2,132	426	20.0%	320	75.1%	$1,689,890	$393,859	23.3%	$309,133	78.5%

(P)—Positive confirmation sent

Note 1: Alternative work was performed on all non-replies

Note 2: No exceptions of audit significance were noted either on the replies or as a result of the alternative test work

Examination of Revenue Cycle - Sales, Cost of Sales, Accounts Receivable

Company __Olde Oak Framing Supplies__   **Period ended** 12/31/77

Item No	Auditing Procedure	Period and Extent	Done By
	The objectives of our audit of the revenue cycle are to ascertain that there is:	Noted	
	• Proper recording of items shipped as sales and proper period cutoff.		JT
	• Proper matching of sales and cost of sales.		JT
	• Propriety and collectibility of accounts receivable balances and proper period cutoff.		JT
	If, after the system has been tested and evaluated we determine that the system is not functioning as effectively as anticipated, the originally designed substantive procedures will be appropriately modified and documented.		JT
	Interim Examinations		
E-1	Familiarize yourself with the client's revenue cycle procedures by reviewing the flowcharts, narratives and bridging workpapers developed during the fieldwork planning phase of the audit.		JT
E-2	Test for numerical sequence of sales invoices:		
	a. Review unissued sales invoices for sequence.		TM
	b. Randomly select__3__months during the year, and		TM
	• Obtain the monthly reconciliations for the numerical sequence of the prenumbered sales invoices. These reconciliations help ensure that all invoices for goods shipped are forwarded for processing.		TM
	• Examine the reconciliation for propriety and note follow-ups of old outstanding invoices.		TM
	• Review the numerical sales invoices file for the same __3__ months for sequence.		TM
	c. On a surprise basis for _One_ day(s)		
	• Review the packing slip file of the dispatcher for numerical sequence. Note any missing packing slips in the file and determine the reason for such missing packing slips.		DS
	• Review the numerical sequence file in the general office for invoices over __30__ days old and determine if follow-up action has been taken		DS
E-4	By observation and inquiry, determine if sales invoices are for merchandise shipped from the warehouse.		DS
E-5	Randomly select__150__packing slips in the dispatcher's file and:		
	a. Trace to the corresponding processed invoice.		
	b. Agree types and quantities of goods shipped to types and quantities billed to customer.		

Examination of Revenue Cycle - Sales, Cost of Sales, Accounts Receivable

Company   Olde Oak Framing Supplies   **Period ended** 12/31/77

Item No.	Auditing Procedure	Period And Extent	Done By
E-6	For the period after installation of the control, use ATTSAMP with a 95% confidence level and a 5% upper precision limit to select a minimum sample of 59 invoices and perform the following: a. Determine that second clerk has initialed the invoice to indicate that control step of checking extensions and prices has been performed. b. For the same 59 invoices, compare billing prices on the invoices to selling prices in effect at invoice date. c. For the same 59 invoices, check extensions and footing totals. d. Prepare a memo documenting the degree of reliance that can be placed on the control in designing other substantive tests.		TM TM
E-9	Randomly select 100 invoices from the numerical invoice trace the totals to the accounts receivable file and records.		

E-10	Confirmation of accounts receivable will be done as of 10/31/77 . If compliance testing indicates weaknesses in controls affecting validity of accounts receivable balances, notify the in-charge accountant immediately.
	
	• Using the firm's computer audit package, perform the following:
	
	  a. Prepare and foot a detailed listing of accounts receivable as of confirmation date.
	
	  b. Reconcile with the general ledger.
	
	  c. Prepare positive confirmation as follows:
	    1. All accounts over sixty days past due.
	    2. All accounts over $2500.
	    3. All accounts of the remaining number.
	
	Note: We have in our possession a magnetic tape of Olde Oak accounts receivable at 10/31/77 which can be used for the above operations.
	
	• Check replies to confirmations and investigate all exceptions.
	
	• Second requests should be sent on positive confirmations for which no replies are received within two weeks.
	
	• Investigate all undelivered requests returned by post office. If possible, obtain better addresses and remail. Apply alternative auditing procedures to requests which cannot be delivered and to positive requests for which no replies are received.		

PROCEDURE	PERSONNEL	GENERAL OFFICE

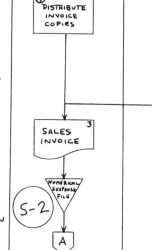

① ALL ORDERS ARE EITHER RECEIVED IN THE MAIL OR PHONED IN BY THE CUSTOMER. PROCEDURES ARE THE SAME FOR EITHER METHOD. ORDER IS ENTERED ON A THREE-PART, PRE-NUMBERED SALES INVOICE. APPROXIMATELY 20,000 INVOICES ARE PROCESSED ANNUALLY. INVOICES ARE ISSUED SEQUENTIALLY.

Personnel: ANY AVAILABLE CLERK

② IF CUSTOMER IS NEW OR ON "WATCH CREDIT" LIST, MANAGER OR ASSISTANT MANAGER MUST APPROVE CREDIT; OTHERWISE INVOICE IS INITIALLED AND FORWARDED.

Personnel: MANAGER'S SECRETARY

③ GET CREDIT BUREAU REPORT. IF CREDIT IS NOT APPROVED, CUSTOMER IS CONTACTED AND OTHER TERMS ARE ARRANGED OR INVOICE IS VOIDED. INVOICE IS INITIALLED AND FORWARDED.

Personnel: MANAGER OR ASSISTANT MANAGER

④ DISTRIBUTE INVOICE COPIES:

No. 1 AND No. 2 ARE GIVEN TO THE WAREHOUSE FOREMAN WHO ASSIGNS WAREHOUSEMEN TO FILL ORDERS.

Personnel: CLERK #1

No. 3 IS FILED NUMERICALLY. FILE IS REVIEWED MONTHLY. OLDER UNMATCHED INVOICES ARE DISCUSSED WITH THE DISPATCHER.

⑤ ORDERS ARE FILLED BY WAREHOUSEMEN, USING INVOICE COPIES. ITEMS SHORT OR NOT IN STOCK ARE LINED OUT. FILLING ORDER INCLUDES COMPLETE PREPARATION FOR SHIPPING. METHOD OF SHIPPING DEPENDS ON SIZE AND WEIGHT OF SHIPMENT. FILLING ORDER ALSO INCLUDES PREPARATION OF PACKING SLIP. PACKING SLIP ASSIGNED SAME NUMBER AS INVOICE.

Personnel: WAREHOUSE FOREMAN AND WAREHOUSEMEN

Flowchart (General Office column):
- CUSTOMER PHONE CALL OR MAIL ORDER
- ① PREPARE THREE-PART SALES INVOICE
- S-1
- ④ DISTRIBUTE INVOICE COPIES
- SALES INVOICE 3
- NUMERICAL SUSPENSE FILE
- S-2
- A — TO 1-2

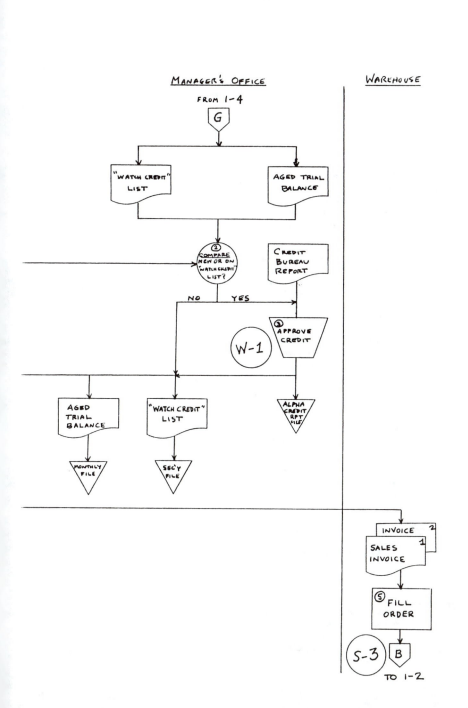

MANAGER'S OFFICE

WAREHOUSE

FROM 1-4

G

"WATCH CREDIT" LIST

AGED TRIAL BALANCE

② COMPARE NEW OR ON "WATCH CREDIT" LIST?

CREDIT BUREAU REPORT

NO   YES

W-1

③ APPROVE CREDIT

AGED TRIAL BALANCE

"WATCH CREDIT" LIST

ALPHA CREDIT RPT FILE

MONTHLY FILE

SEC'Y FILE

INVOICE 2
SALES INVOICE 1

⑤ FILL ORDER

S-3   B

TO 1-2

Olde Oake Framing Supplies	W.P. No.	1-2
Evaluation of Internal Control–Revenue Cycle	Accountant	JT
Sales, Cost of Sales, Accounts Receivable	Date	6/29/76
~~12/31/76~~ 12/31/77	Reviewed	7/15/76 JT

PROCEDURE	PERSONNEL	WAREHOUSE

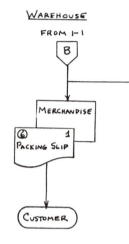

FROM I-1

B

MERCHANDISE

⑥   1
PACKING SLIP

CUSTOMER

⑥ ONE COPY OF PACKING SLIP IS INCLUDED WITH MERCHANDISE BEING SENT TO CUSTOMER. — DISPATCHER

⑦ MATCH CORRECTED INVOICE COPIES No. 1 AND No. 2 WITH FINAL PACKING SLIP PREPARED BY WAREHOUSEMEN. INVOICE COPIES ARE RETURNED TO THE GENERAL OFFICE. — DISPATCHER

⑧ MATCH INVOICE COPIES No. 1 AND No. 2 RECEIVED FROM DISPATCHER WITH CONTROL COPY No. 3. LINE OUT SHORT OR OUT-OF-STOCK ITEMS ON COPY No. 3. PREPARE "OUT-OF-STOCK" REPORT FOR MANAGER TO USE IN PURCHASING DECISIONS. — CLERK #1

⑨ PRICE AND EXTEND ALL THREE INVOICE COPIES FOR DELIVERED ITEMS USING THE MOST CURRENT SELLING PRICES. THESE ARE KEPT IN A LOOSE-LEAF NOTE-BOOK FOR GENERAL OFFICE USE. — CLERK #1

⑩ DISTRIBUTE INVOICE COPIES: — CLERK #3

No. 1 - BATCH FILE
No. 2 - CUSTOMER SUSPENSE FILE
No. 3 - NUMERICAL FILE

IF AN INVOICE IS VOIDED, COPY No. 2 IS FILED WITH COPY No. 3 AND COPY No. 1 IS INCLUDED WITH OTHERS IN BATCH FILE.

⑪ AT THE END OF EACH MONTH, MISSING INVOICES ARE ACCOUNTED FOR, A RECONCILIATION IS PREPARED AND FOLLOW-UP ON MISSING INVOICES IS DOCUMENTED. — CLERK #2

⑪A A SECOND CLERK CHECKS PRICES TO A SEPARATELY MAINTAINED LOOSE-LEAF NOTEBOOK AND ALSO CHECKS EXTENSIONS AND FOOTING. THIS STEP WAS ADDED AS A RESULT OF THE 12/31/76 MANAGEMENT LETTER. CLERK #3 INITIALS INVOICE AFTER CHECKING. — CLERK #3

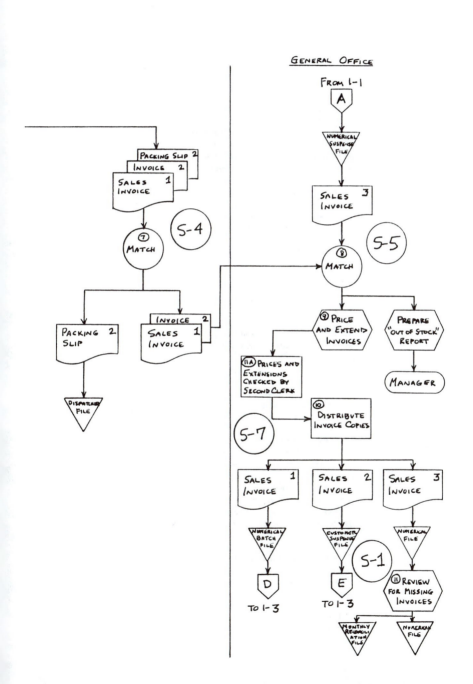

GENERAL OFFICE

FROM 1-1

A

NUMERICAL
SUSPENSE
FILE

SALES   3
INVOICE

⑧
MATCH   S-5

PACKING SLIP 2
INVOICE   2
SALES   1
INVOICE

⑦
MATCH   S-4

INVOICE   2
SALES   1
INVOICE

PACKING   2
SLIP

DISPATCHED
FILE

⑨ PRICE
AND EXTEND
INVOICES

PREPARE
"OUT OF STOCK"
REPORT

MANAGER

⑪A PRICES AND
EXTENSIONS
CHECKED BY
SECOND CLERK

⑩
DISTRIBUTE
INVOICE COPIES

S-7

SALES   1
INVOICE

SALES   2
INVOICE

SALES   3
INVOICE

NUMERICAL
BATCH
FILE

CUSTOMER
SUSPENSE
FILE

NUMERICAL
FILE

D

TO 1-3

E

TO 1-3

S-1

⑪ REVIEW
FOR MISSING
INVOICES

MONTHLY
RECONCILI-
ATION
FILE

NUMERICAL
FILE

PROCEDURE   PERSONNEL

(12) Invoices are sent to data
processing every 2-3 days in   Clerk #2
batches of 100. Before sending,
the clerk prepares an adding
machine tape of the invoices and
attaches it to the top invoice,
along with a notation of the
range of invoice numbers in
the batch. The batch is not
all-inclusive of the numbers
within this range because
processing of orders is not
necessarily sequentially
completed.

(13) Record date and total amounts
of invoices sent to data processing.   Clerk #2
This is written in a small "sales
book" kept by the manager. He
uses it only to "know where he
stands" on sales from day-to-day.

(14) Data processing procedures are
flowcharted separately. Data   Data
processing internal controls   Processing
are evaluated in conjunction
with those flowcharts. *

(15) Upon receipt of the statements
and aged trial balance, the   Clerk #4
clerk matches sales invoices
from customer suspense file
with the statements and
attaches them with envelopes
to the statements. She then
gives the assembled statements
and trial balance to the manager.

At the end of each month,
unmatched invoices in the
customer suspense file are
investigated.

* Not included as a part of
this exercise

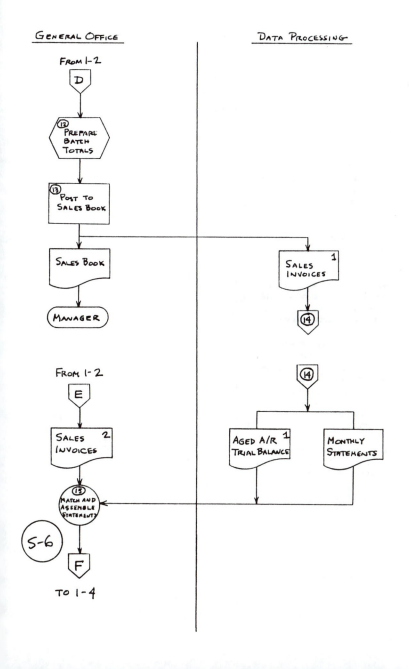

PROCEDURE	PERSONNEL	GENERAL OFFICE

(16) MANAGER REVIEWS ALL ACCOUNTS. HE SPOT-CHECKS SOME STATEMENTS TO THE TRIAL BALANCE AND SOME ATTACHMENTS TO THE STATEMENTS. DURING HIS REVIEW, HE MAKES GENERAL INFORMATION NOTES AND NOTES FOR FOLLOW-UP CALLS TO CUSTOMERS FOR COLLECTION, CREDIT LIMIT, ETC. THESE NOTES ARE DESTROYED AFTER HE FEELS THEY ARE NO LONGER NEEDED.

MANAGER

DURING HIS REVIEW, THE MANAGER ALSO:

(17) UPDATES A LIST OF CUSTOMERS TO "WATCH CREDIT" ON. HE GIVES THIS TO HIS SECRETARY, WHO WILL NOTIFY HIM WHEN ONE OF THESE CUSTOMERS PLACES AN ORDER.

MANAGER

(18) PREPARES A LIST OF ACCOUNTS TO BE WRITTEN OFF AS UNCOLLECTIBLE, AND ATTACHES DOCUMENTATION OF COLLECTION EFFORTS; WRITES EXPLANATIONS FOR ALL ACCOUNTS OVER SIXTY DAYS; FORWARDS REPORT TO CONTROLLER.

MANAGER

(19) PLACES MONTHLY STATEMENTS AND INVOICE COPIES IN ENVELOPES AND MAILS TO CUSTOMERS.

CLERK #4

(20) SEE W/P 1-5 FOR NARRATIVE ON BAD DEBT REVIEW AND WRITE-OFF.

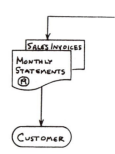

SALES INVOICES

MONTHLY STATEMENTS
(A)

CUSTOMER

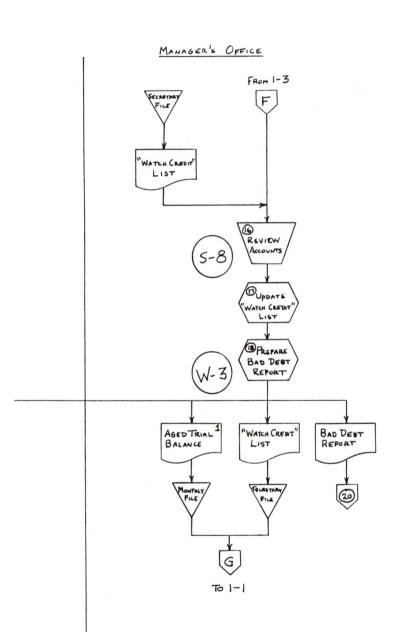

MANAGER'S OFFICE

FROM 1-3

F

SECRETARY FILE

"WATCH CREDIT" LIST

S-8

16 REVIEW ACCOUNTS

17 UPDATE "WATCH CREDIT" LIST

18 PREPARE BAD DEBT REPORT

W-3

AGED TRIAL BALANCE [1]

"WATCH CREDIT" LIST

BAD DEBT REPORT

MONTHLY FILE

SECRETARY FILE

20

G

TO 1-1

Olde Oake Framing Supplies	W.P. No.	2-1
Evaluation of Internal Control–Revenue Cycle	Accountant	JT
Sales, Cost of Sales, Accounts Receivable	Date	6/29/76
12/31/76 ~~12/31/76~~ 12/31/77	Reviewed	7/15/76 JT

AUDIT OBJECTIVES	REF.	INTERNAL CONTROL STRENGTHS
1. PROPER RECORDING OF ITEMS SHIPPED AS SALES AND PROPER PERIOD CUT-OFF.	S-1	PRENUMBERED SALES INVOICES ARE: 1) PREPARED FOR ALL SALES 2) ISSUED SEQUENTIALLY 3) NUMERICALLY ACCOUNTED FOR
	S-2	AFTER SALES INVOICES ARE INITIALLED, ONE COPY IS KEPT IN THE NUMERICAL SUSPENSE FILE UNTIL OTHER COPIES OF THE INVOICE ARE RETURNED FROM THE WAREHOUSE.
	S-3	SALES INVOICES ARE REQUIRED FOR WAREHOUSE PERSONNEL TO FILL AN ORDER.
	S-4	DISPATCHER MAKES CORRECTED SALES INVOICE WITH PACKING SLIP OF MERCHANDISE SHIPPED.
	S-5	THE GENERAL OFFICE CLERK MATCHES COPIES No. 1 AND No 2 OF SALES INVOICES RECEIVED FROM THE DISPATCHER WITH THE CONTROL COPY No 3. THE NUMERICAL SUSPENSE FILE IS PERIODICALLY REVIEWED FOR UNDELIVERED ORDERS.
	S-7	AN INDEPENDENT CLERK CHECKS PRICING OF INVOICE ITEMS AND ALSO CHECKS EXTENSIONS AND FOOTING.

Internal Control Weaknesses	Audit Implications	Audit Procedures	
		Interim	Final
	THIS HELPS ENSURE THAT INVOICES ARE NOT LOST OR MISUSED AND THEY ARE FORWARDED FOR TIMELY PROCESSING	2 3a 3b	13
	BASED ON THE FLOW OF INVOICE COPIES, THERE WOULD HAVE TO BE AT LEAST TWO PEOPLE INVOLVED FOR MERCHANDISE TO LEAVE THE WAREHOUSE AND ALL INVOICE RECORDS TO BE LOST. THIS SEPARATION HELPS ENSURE THAT INVOICES DON'T GET MISPLACED OR MISAPPLIED AND THAT ORDERS ARE NOT SHIPPED WITHOUT AN INVOICE RECORD. PROCESSING ERRORS COULD STILL OCCUR BUT THE OPPORTUNITY FOR INTENTIONAL MISAPPLICATION IS GREATLY REDUCED.	3c	
	THIS PROCEDURE HELPS ENSURE THAT ALL CUSTOMER ORDERS FILLED ARE DOCUMENTED AND CAN BE PROCESSED ON A TIMELY BASIS.	4	
	THIS ENSURES THAT THE SALES INVOICE IS AN ACCURATE REPRESENTATION OF WHAT MERCHANDISE WAS ACTUALLY SHIPPED.	5	
	THIS PROCEDURE HELPS ENSURE THAT ORDERS HAVE BEEN SHIPPED AND RECORDED	3c	
	THIS HELPS ENSURE THAT CUSTOMER IS BILLED THE PROPER AMOUNT AND THAT RECEIVABLE CORRESPONDS TO GOODS SHIPPED.	6	

Olde Oake Framing Supplies	W.P. No.	2-2
Evaluation of Internal Control–Revenue Cycle	Accountant	JT
Sales, Cost of Sales, Accounts Receivable	Date	6/29/76
~~12/31/76~~ 12/31/77	Reviewed	7/15/76 JT

AUDIT OBJECTIVES	REF.	INTERNAL CONTROL STRENGTHS
2. PROPRIETY AND COLLECTIBILITY OF ACCOUNTS RECEIVABLE BALANCES AND PROPER PERIOD CUT-OFF	W-1	
	S-6	THE SALES INVOICE CUSTOMER SUSPENSE FILE IS REVIEWED MONTHLY FOR UNMATCHED INVOICES
	W-3	
	S-8	THE MANAGER REVIEWS MONTHLY STATEMENTS AND ATTACHED INVOICES AND SPOT-CHECKS SOME TO THE AGED TRIAL BALANCE

Internal Control Weaknesses	Audit Implications	Audit Procedures	
		Interim	Final
The manager prepares the "watch credit" list and also approves extension of credit	We cannot rely on the "watch credit" list as a control to prevent sales to known bad accounts		15
	This helps ensure that: 1. All invoices sent to data processing were processed timely, 2. A monthly customer statement was prepared; and 3. Sales invoices appear on the aged trial balance.	7	
The manager approves credit and also prepares the list of accounts receivable to be written off.	We cannot be sure that bad accounts have been written off, particularly those less than sixty days old.		15
	This helps ensure the accuracy and completeness of the monthly statements and aged trial balance.	8	

Objectives

Olde Oak Framing Supplies has not been aggressive in recent years in expanding to new product lines or seeking an expanded customer base. The main objective appears to be to maintain status quo in relationship to competitors by providing quality products and services to their existing customers.

Ownership

Olde Oak Framing Supplies is primarily family owned. Andrew Cole, son of the founder of the company, is President and Chairman of the Board and is also the majority shareholder (60%). Other major shareholders are Stephanie Andrews, his sister, who is on the Board of Directors and Richard Liggett, the family and business attorney. Each owns 12% of-the outstanding shares. The remaining 16% of shares outstanding are owned by various employees who have purchased through a company purchase plan.

Accounting System

The company has an IBM System 3 mini-computer on which they maintain inventory, accounts receivable, payroll, and the general ledger. The computer also prepares monthly invoices, a monthly print-out of the general ledger, and a monthly aging of accounts receivable ("Watch Credit" list).

Management

Key management personnel are all college educated and exhibit a high degree of business knowledge. Andrew Cole, President, has a BBA and worked at all levels of the business when his father was President. Theodore Jones, Controller, has an MBA and is knowledgeable about the EDP system. He has been with the company ten years. Jack Zachery, Vice President, has a BBA and directs the marketing needs of the company.

Audit Completion Requirements

Our audit firm, _____, has been engaged to report on the financial statements of Olde Oak Framing Supplies for the year ended December 31, 1977. One use of the report will be to aid in seeking financing for construction of new facilities in a recently opened industrial park. New facilities are required because of the age and location of the current facilities. The Board of Directors would like the report to be presented to them on March 15, 1978. To meet this deadline, the report must be in printing by approximately February 28, 1978.

Audit Personnel

The audit personnel are:

Partner-in-charge	J. Abbott
Engagement Manager	W. Barnes
Senior	John Thomas
Computer Audit Specialist	B. Rogers
Statistical Audit Specialist	E. Summers
Tax	P. Baca

The total staff time for this year's examination should approximate 600 hours.

Critical Audit and Accounting Areas

Accounts receivable and inventories continue to be critical audit areas, representing 24.0% and 26.0%, respectively, of total assets at September 30, 1977.

Internal Auditor Involvement

Historically, the internal auditor, Paul Jones, has been our liaison with the various client personnel. We reviewed the internal audit function in accordance with auditing standards and concluded that we would rely on the work of the internal auditor. Accordingly, he will assist us in the following areas:

1. Cash balances
2. Accounts receivable confirmation control and follow-up under close supervision.
3. Vouching fixed asset additions and deletions.
4. Coordination of search for unrecorded liabilities.

Audit Schedule

As in the past, client assistance will be used in connection with the preparation of schedules and working papers. Internal audit will coordinate and assign the responsibility of completing audit analysis schedules to other accounting staff members, based on the individual's account responsibility.

1. Interim should accomplish the following items:
    a. Detail review of internal controls, including the data processing system.
    b. Compliance tests of identified strengths of the revenue and purchasing cycles.
    c. Schedule the year-end inventory observations.
    d. Schedule the search for unrecorded liabilities.
    e. Execute the confirmation of accounts receivable.
    f. Perform other substantive tests of the revenue and purchasing cycles as considered necessary.
    g. Tests of fixed asset transactions.

All possible auditing will be performed on the September 30 balances with a roll forward at final.

2. The final examination work will consist of performing and following up any detail test work not completed at the interim examination, testing final balances on accounts verified as of interim dates (to include a review of the roll-forward period) and verifying any remaining account balances that we could not audit at interim. Accounts that will be reviewed as of December 31, 1977 are as follows:

    a. Inventory:

    - Observing physical inventories.
    - Price testing.
    - Testing cut-off procedures.

    b. Accounts payable:
    - Searching for unrecorded liabilities.
    - Testing items vouchered for propriety.

Management letter comments will be reviewed with the respective responsible personnel with their names included on the distribution of copies. Copies of all comments will be left with client personnel.

Miscellaneous Items

Cost of sales is estimated monthly on the basis of samples drawn from the prior month's sales. Cost of sales is adjusted to actual as a result of the annual physical inventory adjustment.

The monthly sample consists of the highest dollar amount invoice from each batch processed. A copy of the invoice in the batch with the highest total dollar amount is made. These copies are forwarded to the purchasing clerk who determines the actual cost of the items sold using the most recent purchase prices available.

At the end of the month, the "costed" copies are forwarded to the controller. Using the ratio of sample invoice cost to sample invoice sales, a clerk estimates cost of sales and makes the appropriate journal entry.

Olde Oak Framing Supplies
Comparative Balance Sheet Analysis
12/31/77

Assets	9/30/77	9/30/76
Current assets:		
Cash	$ 354,600	$ 336,870
Accounts receivable	1,778,832	1,689,890
Inventory	1,927,068	1,830,715
Prepaid expenses	27 300	25,935
Total current assets	4,087,800	3,883,410
Property, plant and equipment:		
Land	875,900	875,900
Buildings and improvements	2,713,300	2,624,135
Automobiles and trucks	135,300	124,400
Furniture and fixtures	880,800	750,500
	4,605,300	4,375,035
Less accumulated depreciation	1,316,900	1,124,100
Net property, plant and equipment	3,288,400	3,250,935
Other assets	35,600	33,400
	$7,411,800	$7,167,745

Liabilities and Stockholders' Equity

Current liabilities:		
Notes payable to bank	$ 800,000	$ 725,000
Current installments of long-term debt	225,000	225,000
Accounts payable	731,900	534,000
Accrued expenses	176,800	118,800
Income taxes	64,300	32,800
Total current liabilities	1,998,000	1,636,000
Long-term debt, excluding current installments	3,010,000	3,235,000
Stockholders' equity:		
Common stock	500,000	500,000
Retained earnings	1,903,800	1,796,745
Total stockholders' equity	2,403,800	2,296,745
	$7,411,800	$7,167,745

Olde Oak Framing Supplies
Comparative Income Statement Analysis
12/31/77

	Nine Months Ended	
	9/30/77	9/30/76
Net sales	$6,875,000	$6,531,250
Cost of sales	4,812,500	4,571,875
Gross profit	2,062,500	1,959,375
Selling, general and		
administrative expenses	1,546,600	1,463,625
Operating income	515,900	495,750
Other income (deductions):		
Interest expense	(74,300)	(59,800)
Other, net	15,400	1,800
	(58,900)	(61,600)
Earnings before income taxes	457,000	434,150
Income taxes	160,000	157,150
Net earnings	297,000	271,000
Retained earnings,		
beginning of period	1,636,800	1,539,745
Dividends paid	(30,000)	(20,000)
Retained earnings,		
end of period	$1,903,800	$1,796,745

Appendix B

Example of Sample Size Rationale Documentation Checklist

Audit Procedure _____

1. Check appropriate objective(s) of the audit procedure.

a. __ This is a substantive test that tests for
   __ The validity of recorded transactions (balances).
   __ The proper authorization of transactions (balances).
   __ The assignment of a proper initial economic value to a transaction (balance) for purposes of recording.
   __ The accurate recording of transactions (balances).
   __ The accurate recording of transactions (balances) toreflect current economic value.

b. __ This is a compliance test that tests for
   __ Control over validity of recorded transactions (balances).
   __ Control over proper authorization of transactions (balances).
   __ Control over assignment of a proper initial economic value.
   __ Control over accuracy of recording of transactions (balances).
   __ Control over proper valuation of transactions (balances).

Note: If the test has dual purposes, check appropriate boxes in both (a) and (b).

2. Check the kind(s) of audit risk this procedure is designed to identify.
   __ Overstatement of account balance
   __ Understatement of account balance
   __ Accounting control deficiency
   __ Other (specify)_____

3. Specify an approximate range of sample sizes you are considering.

   __ The largest sample size you would propose if all factors pointed to a large sample size
   __ The smallest sample size you would propose if all factors pointed to a small sample size and you still decide to perform the procedure.

4. If this is a substantive procedure, what is the measure of materiality of the account balance this procedures relates to?
   __ Highly material
   __ Somewhat material
   __ Immaterial

5. Check any documented internal control strengths that relate to the objective(s) identified in (1) above. | Summarize results (if completed) of compliance tests of controls checked at left.

___ S-1
___ S-2
___ S-3
___ S-4
___ S-5
___ S-6
___ S-7
___ S-8
___ Other (specify)

6. In recommending a sample size, how much reliance are you placing on internal controls?

I_____I_____I_____I
None   Some   Sub-   Very
                 stantial   great

7. Check and scale those factors that apply to the nature of the population.

___ Variability (dispersion) of dollar amounts

I_____I_____I_____I
Low   High

___ Expected error frequency

I_____I_____I_____I
Low   High

___ Expected error magnitude

I_____I_____I_____I
Small   Large

8. Specify other factors that may have an influence on your sample size decision.

   a. Cost/benefit

      ___ More economical procedures are available that would gather similar evidence (specify below).

      ___ Other procedures are available that would gather more evidence at the same cost (specify below).

      ___ Other (specify below).

b. Results of other audit procedures.

___ Other tests performed this year (specify below).

___ Tests performed in prior year (specify below).

c. Other (specify).

9. Describe briefly how you plan to evaluate the results of this procedure (e.g., what effect will errors have on the evaluation; what kinds of conclusions can be reached?).

10. Describe briefly how you combined the preceding factors to reach a sample size decision.

11. Explain your recommended sample size.

Appendix C

Figure C.1
Sample Size Recommendations for Audit Procedure
E-5, Packing Slip Comparison

Control Treatment	No Guidance	Narrative Guidance	Structured Guidance	Statistical Approach	Manager Review
Fair	50	50	60	0	50
	150	150	40	300	50
	100	59	100	59	150
	0	0	59	100	50
	59	300	100	59	0
	0	0	150	150	0
	59	50	75	50	0
	200	300	80	100	150
	75	50	60	60	100
	60	75	30	65	65
	0	0	0	392	120
	0	40	50	0	59
	150	59	60	0	100
	100	59	75	0	75
	200	50	100	150	75
	50	150	75	0	
	25	100	0	0	
	75	50	150		
	50				
Strong	30	100	75	0	59
	70	0	100	59	59
	0	59	100	99	59
	59	0	30	150	59
	59	0	200	59	59
	59	59	60	400	59
	50	50	75	0	59
	150	25	69	0	59
	0	30	0	59	60
	59	50	60	65	200
	50	59	0	75	59
	59	84	100	150	75
	0	54	50	0	40
	79	75	125	65	10
	60	75	60	59	100
	75	50	0	0	
	59	150	100	150	
	59	83			

Note that zero entries represent either that the step was eliminated or that no explicit scope recommendation was made (i.e., a missing observation).

Figure C.2
Sample Size Recommendations for Audit Procedure
E-6b, c, Pricing Test

Control Treatment	Guidance Treatment				
	No Guidance	Narrative Guidance	Structured Guidance	Statistical Approach	Manager Review
Fair	100	83	59	0	59
	59	71	35	149	0
	100	59	10	59	88
	59	75	0	100	59
	59	300	8 0	59	250
	100	100	59	0	0
	59	79	59	59	59
	200	90	0	65	59
	75	79	59	65	65
	75	75	135	65	59
	0	80	0	59	59
	59	59	59	116	59
	150	67	59	0	100
	59	0	59	59	75
	100	0	59	59	75
	75	75	75	0	
	59	75	0	0	
	0	75	75		
	40				
Strong	30	59	25	59	59
	75	0	50	121	59
	109	59	15	99	59
	59	20	0	150	59
	59	0	59	59	59
	59	59	75	149	59
	59	50	59	0	59
	0	25	69	65	59
	0	20	0	59	45
	59	59	59	65	0
	59	59	0	24	59
	59	59	59	65	40
	0	59	30	0	25
	59	45	59	65	20
	60	59	59	59	59
	59	100	59	59	
	59	59	59	59	
	59	59	59		

Note that zero entries represent either that the step was eliminated or that no explicit scope recommendation was made (i.e., a missing observation).

Figure C.3
Sample Size Recommendations for Audit Procedure E-9, Posting Test

	Guidance Treatment				
Control Treatment	No Guidance	Narrative Guidance	Structured Guidance	Statistical Approach	Manager Review
Fair	50	25	80	150	75
	59	100	0	300	75
	100	59	25	59	100
	30	25	20	100	100
	59	300	59	100	0
	100	0	100	100	250
	59	59	0	200	0
	200	0	0	65	59
	0	59	59	100	100
	0	0	100	0	65
	0	0	0	392	100
	0	59	59	0	75
	150	59	100	0	75
	59	45	50	0	75
	50	100	0	150	0
	50	0	0	0	
	0	50	0	0	
	0	0	100		
	25				
Strong	30	0	0	0	59
	33	0	75	59	59
	50	0	40	99	50
	59	0	25	60	59
	60	0	0	0	0
	59	0	75	300	59
	50	0	30	0	59
	0	25	59	0	59
	50	10	0	59	60
	59	59	59	65	200
	60	0	0	25	59
	0	59	100	100	50
	0	59	150	0	20
	25	50	59	65	10
	0	50	0	0	80
	75	0	250	0	
	100	0	50	100	
	59	59			

Note that zero entries represent either that the step was eliminated or that no explicit scope recommendation was made (i.e., a missing observation).

Figure C.4
Sample Size Recommendations for Total Confirmations
(Positives Plus Negatives)
for Audit Procedure E-10, Confirmations

Control Treatment	Guidance Treatment				
	No Guidance	Narrative Guidance	Structured Guidance	Statistical Approach	Manager Review
Fair	547	515	405	513	392
	352	439	480	915	0
	0	316	394	0	439
	501	195	350	601	275
	439	439	149	427	425
	364	300	515	915	194
	294	0	475	226	394
	410	394	0	314	335
	316	649	400	361	369
	249	438	0	243	316
	475	265	439	392	370
	615	979	200	915	150
	154	297	294	775	694
	502	0	0	915	294
	500	439	0	0	300
	491	0	325	0	
	420	420	0	0	
	271	275	630		
	194	0	0		
Strong	276	385	160	904	439
	125	230	439	0	0
	316	135	494	0	244
	394	191	394	0	300
	314	0	439	341	319
	556	0	161	551	276
	349	194	0	287	235
	244	349	375	601	159
	0	399	149	221	232
	479	439	439	359	269
	260	439	241	180	271
	207	382	400	784	345
	276	225	0	0	316
	300	439	200	314	0
	297	244	240	668	319
	0	200	320	629	
	194	294	417	466	
	253	0			

Note that zero entries represent either that the step was eliminated or that no explicit scope recommendation was made (i.e., a missing observation).

Bibliography

American Accounting Association. *Report of the 1976-77 Committee on Human Information Processing.* Sarasota, Fla.: American Accounting Association, 1977.

American Institute of Accountants. *Examination of Financial Statements by Independent Public Accountants.* New York: AIA, 1936.

American Institute of Accountants. "Extensions of Auditing Procedure." *Journal of Accountancy* 68 (December 1939): 377-85.

American Institute of Accountants. Statement on Auditing Procedure 5. *The Revised SEC Rule on "Accountants Certificates."* New York: AIA, 1941.

American Institute of Accountants. *Tentative Statement of Auditing Standards - Their Generally Accepted Significance and Scope.* New York: AIA, 1947.

American Institute of Accountants. *Internal Control: Elements of a Coordinated System and Its importance to Management and the Independent Public Accountant.* New York: AIA, 1949.

American Institute of Accountants. Statement on Auditing Procedure 24. *Revision in Short-Form Accountant's Report or Certificate.* New York: AIA, 1948.

American Institute of Certified Public Accountants. Statement on Auditing Procedure 29. *Scope of the Independent Auditor's Review of Internal Control.* New York: AICPA, 1958.

American Institute of Certified Public Accountants. Statement on Auditing Procedure 49. *Reports on Internal Control.* New York: AICPA, 1971.

American Institute of Certified Public Accountants. Statement on Auditing Procedure 52. *Reports on Internal Control Based on Criteria Established by Governmental Agencies.* New York: AICPA, 1972.

American Institute of Certified Public Accountants. Statement on Auditing Procedure 54. *The Auditor's Study and Evaluation of Internal Control.* New York: AICPA, 1972.

American Institute of Certified Public Accountants. Statement on Auditing Standards 1. *Codification of Auditing Standards and Procedures.* New York: AICPA, 1973.

American Institute of Certified Public Accountants. Statement on Auditing Standards 9. *The Effect of an Internal Audit Function on the Scope of the Independent Auditor's Examination.* New York: AICPA, 1975.

American Institute of Certified Public Accountants. Statement on Auditing Standards 20. *Required Communication of Material Weaknesses in Internal Accounting Control.* New York: AICPA, 1977.

American Institute of Certified Public Accountants. Statement on Auditing Standards 31. *Evidential Matter.* New York: AICPA, 1980.

Arens, Alvin A. "The Adequacy of Audit Evidence Accumulation in Public Accounting." Ph.D. dissertation, University of Minnesota, 1970.

Arens, Alvin A. And Loebbecke, James K. *Auditing: An Integrated Approach.* Englewood Cliffs. N.J.: Prentice-Hall, 1976.

Ashton, Robert H. "An Experimental Study of Internal Control Judgments." *Journal of Accounting Research* 12 (Spring 1974): 143-57.

Bamber, E. Michael. *Expert Judgment in the Audit Team: Perception of Judgment Differences.* Unpublished working paper, the faculty of Accounting, The Ohio State University, 1979.

Barrett, Michael J.; Baker, Donald W.; and Ricketts, Donald E. "Internal Control Systems: How to Calculate Incremental Effectiveness and Cost Using Reliability Concepts." *Internal Auditor* 34 (October 1977): 31-43.

Berelson, Bernard. "Content Analysis." In *Handbook of Social Psychology,* ed. Gardner Lindzey, vol. 1, pp. 488-522. Cambridge, Mass.: Addison-Wesley Publishing Co., 1954.

Biggs, Stanley F. "An Investigation of the Decision Processes Underlying the Assessment of Corporate Earning Power." Ph.D. dissertation, University of Minnesota, 1978.

Biggs, Stanley F. and Mock, Theodore J. "An Investigation of Auditor Decision Processes in the Evaluation of Internal Controls and Audit Scope Decisions," *Journal of Accounting Research* (Spring 1983).

Biggs, Stanley F. And Mock, Theodore J. "Criteria Auditors Utilize in the Evaluation of Internal Accounting Control." *Pacific Accounting Review,* 01/89, pp. 59-75.

Bodnar, George. "Reliability Modeling of Internal Control Systems." *Accounting Review* 50 (October 1975): 747-57.

Brown, R. Gene. "Objective Internal Control Evaluation." *Journal of Accountancy* 114 (November 1962): 50-56.

Burns, David C. And Loebbecke, James K. "Internal Control Evaluation: How the computer Can Help." *Journal of Accountancy* 140 (August 1975): 60-70.

Carmichael, Douglas R. "Behavioral Hypotheses of Internal Control." *Accounting Review* 45 (April 1970): 235-45.

Cash, James I., Jr.; Bailey, Andrew D., Jr.; and Whinston, Andrew B. "A Survey of Techniques for Auditing EDP-Based Accounting Information Systems." *Accounting Review* 52 (October 1977): 813-32.

Cash, James I., Jr.; Bailey, Andrew D., Jr.; and Whinston, Andrew B. "The TICOM Model - A Network Data Base Approach to Review and Evaluation of Internal Control Systems." *Proceedings of the American Federation of Information Processing Societies Conference.* Montvale, N.J.: AFIPS, 1977.

Chesley, G. Richard. "Procedures for the Communication of Uncertainty in Auditor's Working Papers. "In *Behavioral Experiments in Accounting II,* ed. Thomas J. Burns. Columbus: The Ohio State University, 1979.

Cohen, Jacob. "A Coefficient of Agreement for Nominal Scales." *Educational and Psychological Measurement* 20 (Spring 1960): 37-46.

Cushing, Barry E. "A Mathematical Approach to the Analysis and Design of Internal Control Systems." *Accounting Review* 49 (January 1974): 24-41.

Einhorn, Hillel J.; Hogarth, Robin M.; and Klempner, Eric. "Quality of Group Judgment." *Psychological Bulletin* 84 (January/February 1977): 158-72.

Elliott, Robert K. And Rogers, John R. "Relating Statistical Sampling to Audit Objectives." *Journal of Accountancy* 134 (July 1972): 46-55.

English, Horace B. And English, Ava Champney. *A Comprehensive Dictionary of Psychological and Psychoanalytical Terms*. New York: Longmans, Green & Co., 1958.

Ericsson, K. Anders and Simon, Herbert A. *Retrospective Verbal Reports as Data*. Complex Information Processing Working Paper 388. Pittsburgh: Carnegie Mellon University, 1978.

Ericsson, K. Anders and Simon, Herbert A. *Thinking-Aloud Protocols as Data: Effects of Verbalization.* Complex Information Processing Working Paper 397. Pittsburgh: Carnegie Mellon University, 1979.

Ericsson, K. Anders and Simon, Herbert A. *Protocol Analysis: Verbal Reports as Data*. Cambridge, Mass.: The MIT Press, 1984.

Federal Reserve Board. *Verification of Financial Statements (Revised)*. Washington, D.C., 1929.

Hofstedt, T. R. And Hughes, G.D. "An Experimental Study of the Judgment Element in Disclosure Decisions." *Accounting Review* 52 (April 1977): 379-95.

Holsti, Ole R. *Content Analysis for the Social Sciences and Humanities*. Reading Mass.: Addison-Wesley Publishing Co., 1969.

Ishikawa, Akira. "A Mathematical Approach to the Analysis and Design of Internal Control Systems: A Brief Comment." *Accounting Review* 50 (January 1975): 148-50.

Joyce, Edward J. "Expert Judgment in Audit Program Planning." *Studies on Human Information Processing in Accounting".* Supp. to vol. 14 of the *Journal of Accounting Research* (1976): 29-60.

Kinney, William R., Jr. "A Decision Theory Approach to the Sampling Problem in Auditing." *Journal of Accounting Research* 13, (Spring 1975): 117-32.

Kinney, William R., Jr. "Decision Theory Aspects of Internal Control System Design/Compliance and Substantive Tests." *Studies on Statistical Methodology in Auditing.* Supp. to vol. 13 of the *Journal of Accounting Research* (1975): 14-29.

Klersey, George F. And Mock, Theodore J. "Verbal Protocol Research in Accounting." *Accounting, Organizations and Society*, vol. 2, no. 1/2 (1989): 133-52.

Libby, Robert and Blashfield, Roger K. "Performance of a Composite as a Function of the Number of Judges." *Organizational Behavior and Human Performance* 21 (April 1978): 121-29.

Libby, Robert and Lewis, Barry L. "Human Information Processing Research in Accounting: The State of the Art." *Accounting, Organizations, and Society*, vol. 2, no. 3 (1977): 245-68.

Lin, W. Thomas, Mock, Theodore J., Newton, Lauren K., and Vasarhelyi, Miklos A. "A Review of Audit Research". *Accounting Journal (forthcoming)*.

Loebbecke, James K. "Discussant's Response to A Decision Theory View of Auditing." In *Contemporary Auditing Problems*, ed. Howard F. Stettler, pp. 720-75. Lawrence, Kansas: University of Kansas Printing Service, 1974.

Loebbecke, James K. "Impact and Implementation of the Auditing Statement on Internal Control." *Journal of Accountancy* 139 (May 1975): 80-83.

Mair, William C.; Wood, Donald R.; and Davis, Keagle W. *Computer Control and Audit*, rev. ed. Altamonte Springs, Florida: Institute of Internal Auditors, 1973.

Mautz, R. K. And Sharaf, Hussein A. *The Philosophy of Auditing*. Menasha, Wisconsin: American Accounting Association, 1961.

Mock, Theodore J.. And Turner, Jerry L. "The Effect of Changes in Internal Controls on Audit Programs." In *Behavioral Experiments in Accounting II*, ed. Thomas J. Burns, pp. 277-321. Columbus: The Ohio State University, 1979.

Montgomery, Robert H. *Auditing: Theory and Practice*. 2d. Ed., rev. and enl. New York: Ronald Press Co., 1917.

Montgomery, Robert H.; Lenhart, N.J.; and Jennings, A.R. *Montgomery's Auditing*. 7th ed. New York: Ronald Press Co., 1979.

Morris, William and Anderson, Hershel. "Audit Scope Adjustments for Internal Control." CPA Journal 46 (July 1976): 15-20.

Newell, Allen and Simon, Herbert. *Human Problem Solving*. Englewood Cliffs, N.J.: Prentice-Hall, 1972.

Nisbett, Richard E. And Wilson, Timothy Decamp. "Telling More than We Can Know: Verbal Reports on Mental Processes." *Psychological Review* 84 (May 1977): 231-59.

Peat, Marwick, Mitchell & Co. *Action Plan for Reviewing Internal Accounting Controls*. New York: Peat, Marwick, Mitchell & Co., 1978.

Peat Marwick, Mitchell & Co. *Research Opportunities in Auditing*. New York: Peat, Marwick, Mitchell & Co., 1976.

Roberts, Donald M. *Statistical Auditing*. New York: AICPA, 1978.

Securities and Exchange Commission Regulation S-X. Form and Content of Financial Statements. Washington, D.C.: U.S. Government Printing Office, 1941, as amended to and including February 5, 1941.

Stratton, W. "Accounting Internal Control Systems: Their Reliability and Dichotomic Structure Functions." Ph.D. dissertation. Claremont Graduate School, 1977.

Swieringa, Robert J. "A Behavioral Approach to Internal Control Evaluation." *Internal Auditor* 29 (March/April 1972): 30-45.

Swieringa, Robert J. "An Inquiry into the Nature and Feasibility of a Sociometric Analysis of Internal Control." Ph.D. dissertation, University of Illinois, 1969.

Swieringa, Robert J. And Carmichael, Douglas R. "A Positional Analysis of Internal Control." *Journal of Accountancy* 131 (February 1979): 34-43.

Turner, Jerry L. And Mock, Theodore J. "Economic Considerations in Designing Audit Programs." *Journal of Accountancy* 149 (March 1980): 65-74.

Tversky, A. And Kahneman, D. "Judgment Under Uncertainty: Heuristics and Biases." *Science* (September 27, 1974): 1124-31.

Weber, Ronald A.G., "Auditor Decision Making: A Study of Some Aspects of Accuracy and Consensus, and the Usefulness of a Simulation Decision Aid for Assessing Overall System Reliability." Ph.D. dissertation, University of Minnesota, 1977.

Willingham, John J. "Internal Control Evaluation - A Behavioral Approach." *Internal Auditor* 23 (Summer 1966): 20-26.

Yu, S. And Neter, J. "A Stochastic Model of the Internal Control System." *Journal of Accounting Research* 11 (Autumn 1973): 273-95.